CW01192451

# Fridtjof Nansen

A book for the young

by
**Jacob B. Bull**

Translated
By the
**Rev. Mordaunt R. Barnard**
Vicar of Margaretting, Essex
One of the translators of Dr. Nansen's "Farthest North"

---

BOSTON, U.S.A.
D. C. HEATH & CO., PUBLISHERS
1903

LEGATUM
PUBLISHING
Identity • History • Knowledge

**2022**

Original:

Fridtjof Nansen A Book for the Young
D.C. Heath & Co, Boston, U.S.A., 1903

Title: Fridtjof Nansen A Book for the Young

Copyright notice. All rights reserved for the foreword and layout. These elements are the property of Legatum Publishing AS and may not be reproduced or utilised in any form or by any means (whether electronic or mechanical), including photocopying, recording or by any information storage retrieval system, without written permission from the publisher.

The rest of the book is public domain and one may freely copy and distribute its contents, as no entity (individual or corporate) holds any copyright over the remaining material.

Author: Jacob B. Bull
Translator: Rev. Mordaunt R. Barnard

Foreword: Bjørn Christian Rødal

ISBN 978-82-93925-09-5

BIC classification: Educational History YQH; Childrens and teenage: general non-fiction YN

Cover Photo: Fridtjof Nansen
George Grantham Bain collection at the Library of Congress

Editor and layout: Richard Krogstad

LEGATUM PUBLISHING AS

www.legatum-publishing.com

# Dedication

Dedicated to the youth of our generation; born too late to explore the earth, too soon to explore the stars; but just in time to explore, secure and expand the European legacy.

# Foreword

This book may serve as a brief introduction to the character of Fridtjof Nansen. It was published in 1898, during Nansen's lifetime, and gives us an insight into how he was viewed already by his contemporaries. It details in a lively manner his childhood and his early life as an athlete, scientist and adventurer. It illustrates the context that would come to shape Nansen's philosophy later in life and give him his direction, both as a humanitarian and as statesman.

The first of Nansen's exploits to earn him renown were his arctic expeditions, first crossing Greenland on ski and later his journey towards the North Pole. To mount a polar expedition today over 125 years later with modern technology, equipment and radio communication is itself a herculean task few men or women could do. But to do so under the conditions Nansen did is even more impressive.

Imagine yourself, standing on the edge of the frozen waste of the North Pole. Ice, snow and biting cold as far as you can see. No radio, no rescue or backup, just you and your wits against the arctic elements. To fail is to die. To an ordinary man the odds would seem insurmountable, leading only to death on the arctic wastes. Indeed, many arctic expeditions had perished previously, leaving Nansen fully aware of the dangers involved. Nansen received a doctorate (PhD) for his dissertation, based on the scientific findings he made during his expeditions.

Nansen's success lay in diligent preparation and meticulous planning. He prepared both his body as well as his mind for this task. His quick wits and resourcefulness as well as personal bravery saved the lives of his expeditioners on several occasions. But above all, like all great men he was first and foremost a man of vision, driven by an indomitable will to persevere and overcome against all odds.

In the years after the publication of this book (1898) Nansen became more publicly active and involved with the larger political questions of his day. Leading up to the separation of the union of Norway and Sweden in

1905, Nansen was a staunch supporter of Norwegian independence, and even wrote a book *Norway and the Union with Sweden*, to promote the case for Norwegian independence abroad. Subsequently Nansen was offered a place in the cabinet of the new government, but declined the offer and served instead in a diplomatic capacity. Nansen received a secret mission to go to Copenhagen and persuade Prince Carl of Denmark to become the new King of Norway. Prince Carl would later take the name Haakon the 7th of Norway, upon ascending the Norwegian throne. Later in 1906 Nansen was appointed as Norway's first ambassador in London.

When the First World War broke out Norway declared a position of neutrality and continued their overseas trade the best they could. But when the United States entered the war in 1917 they placed extra restrictions on international trade and as a result the loss of Norway's overseas trade led to shortages of food in the country. Nansen was dispatched to Washington by the Norwegian government to negotiate terms that would allow supplies into the country. After several months of negotiation he finally secured food and other supplies. When the Norwegian government hesitated over the deal Nansen signed the agreement on his own initiative, in keeping with his decisive character.

Nansen would later go on to lead humanitarian efforts in the aftermath of the First World War. This was yet another daunting undertaking for Nansen to pour his immense energy into. Nansen became engaged with the League of Nations and the repatriation of prisoners of war. In 1920 he began organising the repatriation of about half a million prisoners that were scattered around the world. His arctic expeditions had proven to the world that he was both capable and trustworthy.

Later Nansen was appointed by the League of Nations to the position of High Commissioner for Refugees in 1921, his first task being the resettlement of around two million Russian refugees displaced by the upheavals of the Russian Revolution, many of whom were threatened by starvation and violence. At the same time he tried to tackle the urgent problem of the Russian famine. After widespread crop failures around 30 million people were facing starvation and death.

The horrors of the communist revolution in Russia with the ensuing civil war and the famine made a strong impression on Nansen that would later come to show in his social and political activities towards the end of his life.

When the Greco-Turkish war ended in 1922 Nansen devised a plan for a population exchange whereby half a million Turks in Greece were returned to Turkey, with full financial compensation. The same was done to facilitate the absorption of Greek refugees from Turkey into their homeland.

Nansen was awarded the Nobel Peace Prize for 1922. The prize was given due to *"his work for the repatriation of the prisoners of war, his work for the Russian refugees, his work to bring succour to the millions of Russians afflicted by famine, and finally his present work for the refugees in Asia Minor and Thrace"*.

He also worked hard to raise awareness about the Armenian genocide at the hands of the Turkish government, and the enduring plight of Armenian refugees. Nansen's contribution is still remembered by Armenians to this day.

At home in Norway he was one of the founders of *Fedrelandslaget (National association for the Fatherland)*, a patriotic organisation tasked with the objective of preserving and cultivating Norwegian identity and national interests and to serve as a counter force to the revolutionary labour movement.

Based on his first hand experience of the "red terror" that had taken place in Russia and Ukraine, he warned against the dangers of communism and what he named "class hatred". Nansen called instead for a path of national unity and harmony, advocating for cooperation and solidarity among the different classes in society. In his speech at the founding of *Fedrelandslaget* he addressed this concern, and said that brotherly love and mutual understanding must form the basis of a healthy and functioning society.

Nansen's philosophy combined nationalism with international cooperation and mutual respect between the nations. He thought that all the nations of the world should cultivate their unique culture and heritage, but that all the peoples of the world were also interdependent on each other in a kind of "world organism". If a nation were to disappear the world would become a poorer place and the overall organism would be weakened.

Fridtjof Nansen, the greatest Norwegian of modern times. Adventurer. Scientist. Statesman. Humanitarian. The remarkable life and character of Fridtjof Nansen speaks to us through history. His achievements have made him into a national icon in Norway and known around the world. Through his deeds he has entered into a select group of men and women worthy of praise and remembrance for generations to come.

Bjørn Christian Rødal

Bergen, desember 2021

# Contents

I. Nansen's Boyhood—Education and Character ............... 11

II. Youtful Adventures ............................................. 21

III. Mountain-climbing in Winter .............................. 33

IV. Preparing for the Greenland Expedition .................. 38

V. Sledging across Greenland .................................... 51

VI. Nansen's Marriage—A Strange Wedding-trip ............ 68

VII. The Fram—Setting out for the Pole ...................... 75

VIII. The Ice Pressure—Hunting the White Bear ............ 84

IX. Farthest North ................................................ 97

X. Nansen Meeting Dr. Jackson in Franz Joseph Land ........ 108

Other publications by Legatum Publishing ................. 117

# Illustrations

Map of Nansen's Polar Route ................................................ 10

Store Fröen, Nansen's Birthplace ........................................ 12

Nansen at Nineteen ............................................................ 27

Otto Sverdrup ...................................................................... 44

Camp on the Drift Ice ........................................................ 47

East Greenland Esquimaux ................................................ 55

Sledging Across Greenland ................................................ 61

On the Way To Godthaap .................................................. 64

Crew of the Fram ................................................................ 77

The Fram in an Ice Pressure .............................................. 85

Nansen and Johansen Leaving the Fram .......................... 98

Meeting of Nansen and Jackson ...................................... 109

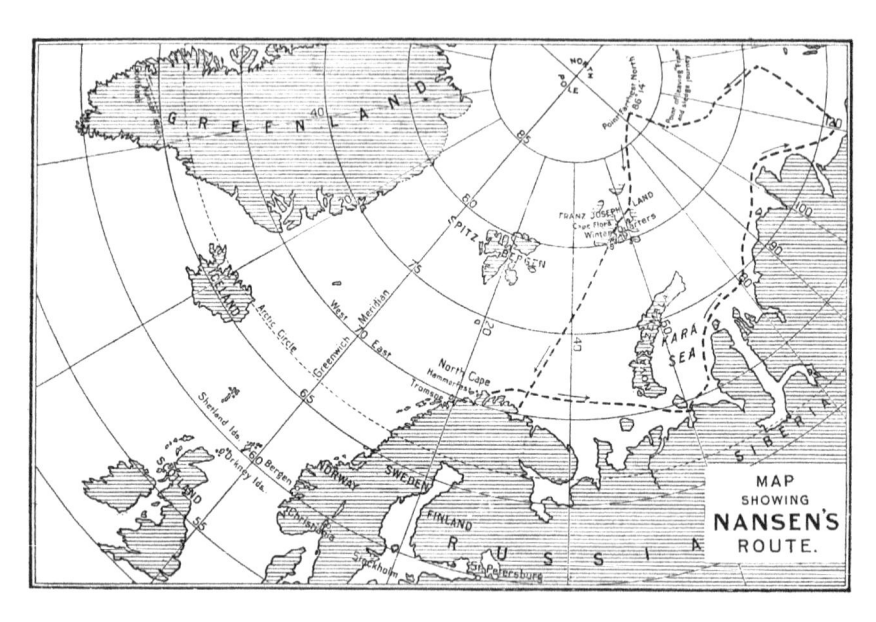

*Map showing Nansen's route.*

# Chapter I

NANSEN'S BOYHOOD—EDUCATION AND CHARACTER

Nansen's Birthplace and Childhood Home.—Burgomaster Nansen, his Ancestor.—His Boyhood and Education.—Early Love of Sport and Independent Research.

In West Aker, a short distance from Christiania, there is an old manor-house called Store Fröen. It is surrounded by a large courtyard, in the middle of which is a dovecot. The house itself, as well as the out-houses, is built in the old-fashioned style. The garden, with its green and white painted fence, is filled with fruit-trees, both old and young, whose pink and snow-white blossoms myriads of bumblebees delight to visit in springtime, while in autumn their boughs are so laden with fruit that they are bent down under a weight they can scarcely support.

Close by the garden runs the Frogner River. Here and there in its course are deep pools, while in other places it runs swiftly along, and is so shallow that it can readily be forded. All around are to be seen in winter snow-covered heights, while far away in the background a dense pine forest extends beyond Frogner Sæter,[1] beyond which again lies Nordmarken, with its hidden lakes, secret brooklets, and devious paths, like a fairy-tale. And yet close by the hum of a busy city life with all its varied sounds may be heard.

It was in this house that, on Oct. 10, 1861, a baby boy, Fridtjof Nansen, was born.

Many years before this, on Oct. 9, 1660, two of Denmark's most powerful men were standing on the castle bridge at Copenhagen eyeing each other with looks of hatred and defiance. One of these, named Otto Krag, was glancing angrily at Blaataarn (the Blue Tower) with its dungeons. "Know you that?" he inquired of his companion, the chief burgomaster of the city. Nodding assent, and directing his looks toward the church tower of "Our Lady," in which were hung the alarm bells, the latter replied, "And know you what hangs within yonder tower?"

Four days later the burghers of Copenhagen, with the burgomaster at their head, overthrew the arrogant Danish nobles, and made Frederick III absolute monarch over Denmark and Norway.

*Store Frøen*

It needed unyielding strength and indomitable courage to carry out such an undertaking, but these were qualifications which the burgomaster possessed, and had at an early age learned to employ. When but sixteen he had set out from Flensborg on an expedition to the White Sea in a vessel belonging to his uncle, and had then alone traversed a great portion of Russia. Four years later he commanded an expedition to the Arctic Ocean, and subsequently entered the service of the Iceland Company as captain of one of their ships.

When forty years of age he was made an alderman of Copenhagen, and in 1654 became its chief burgomaster. During the siege of that city in the war with Charles the Tenth (Gustavus), he was one of its most resolute and intrepid defenders; and so when the power of the Danish nobility was to be overthrown, it was he who took the chief part in the movement.

This man, who was neither cowed by the inherited tyranny of the nobles, nor daunted by the terrors of war or the mighty forces of nature, was named Hans Nansen; and it is from him, on his father's side, that Fridtjof Nansen descended.

---

Our hero's mother is a niece of Count Wedel Jarlsberg, the Statholder[2] of Norway,—the man who in 1814 risked life and fortune to provide Norway with grain from Denmark, and who did his share toward procuring a free and equable union with Sweden.

Fridtjof Nansen grew up at Store Fröen, and it was not long before the strongly marked features of his race became apparent in the fair, shock-haired lad with the large, dark-blue, dreamy eyes.

Whatever was worthy of note, he must thoroughly master; whatever was impossible for others, he must do himself. He would bathe in the Frogner River in spring and autumn in the coldest pools; fish bare-legged with self-made tackle in the swiftest foss;[3] contrive and improve on everything pertaining to tools and implements, and examine and take to pieces all the mechanical contrivances that came in his way; often succeeding, frequently failing, but never giving in.

Once, when only three years old, he was nearly burned to death. He had been meddling with the copper fire in the brewhouse, and was standing in the courtyard busied with a little wheelbarrow. All at once his clothes were on fire, for a spark, it seems, had lighted on them, and from exposure to the air, burst out into flames. Out rushed the housekeeper to the rescue. Meanwhile Fridtjof stood hammering away at his barrow, utterly indifferent to the danger he was in, while the housekeeper was extinguishing the fire. "It was quite enough for one person to see to that sort of thing," he thought.

On one occasion he very nearly caused the drowning of his younger brother in the icy river. His mother appeared on the scene as he was in the act of dragging him up out of the water. She scolded him severely; but the lad tried to comfort her by saying, that "once he himself had nearly been drowned in the same river when he was quite alone."

Once or twice on his early fishing-excursions he managed to get the fishhook caught in his lip, and his mother had to cut it out with a razor, causing the lad a great deal of pain, but he bore it all without a murmur.

The pleasures of the chase, too, were a great source of enjoyment to him in his childish years. At first he would go out after sparrows and squirrels with a bow and arrow like the Indian hunters. Naturally he did not meet with much success. It then occurred to him that a cannon would be an excellent weapon for shooting sparrows. Accordingly he procured one, and after loading it up to the muzzle with gunpowder, fired it off, with the result that the cannon burst into a hundred pieces, and a large part of the charge was lodged in his face, involving the interesting operation of having the grains of powder picked out with a needle.

The system on which the Nansen boys were brought up at Store Fröen was to inure them in both mind and body. Little weight was attached to trivial matters. The mistakes they made they must correct for themselves as far as possible; and if they brought suffering on themselves they were taught to endure it. The principles of self-help were thus inculcated at an early age—principles which they never forgot in later days.

As Fridtjof grew up from the child into the boy, the two opposite sides of his character became apparent,—inflexible determination, and a dreamy love of adventure; and the older he grew, the more marked did these become. He was, as the saying is, "a strange boy." Strong as a young bear, he was ever foremost in fight with street boys, whom he daily met between his home and school. When the humor took him, especially if his younger brother was molested, he would fight fiercely, though the odds were three or four to one against him. But in general, he was of a quiet, thoughtful disposition.

Sometimes indeed he would sit buried in deep thought half an hour at a time, and when dressing would every now and then remain sitting with one stocking on and the other in his hand so long that his brother had to call out to him to make haste. At table, too, he would every now and then forget to eat his food, or else would devour anything and everything that came in his way.

The craving to follow out his own thoughts and his own way thus displayed itself in his early childhood, and he had not attained a great age before his longing to achieve exploits and to test his powers of endurance became apparent.

It began with a pair of ski[4] made by himself for use on the Frogner hills, developed in the hazardous leaps on the Huseby[5] slopes, and culminated in his becoming one of Norway's cleverest and most enduring runners on ski. It began with fishing for troutlets in the river, and ended with catching seals in the Arctic seas. It began with shooting sparrows with cannons, and ended with shooting the polar bear and walrus with tiny Krag-Jörgensen conical bullets. It began with splashing about in the cold pools of the Frogner river, and ended in having to swim for dear life amid the ice floes of the frozen ocean. Persevering and precise, enduring and yet defiant, step by step he progressed.

Nothing was ever skipped over—everything was thoroughly learned and put into practice. Thus the boy produced the man!

There was a certain amount of pride in Fridtjof's nature that under different circumstances might have proved injurious to him. He was proud of his descent, and of his faith in his own powers. But the strict and wise guidance of his parents directed this feeling into one of loyalty—loyalty toward his friends, his work, his plans. His innate pride thus became a conscientious feeling of honor in small things as well as great—a mighty lever, forsooth, to be employed in future exploits.

Meanness was a thing unknown to Fridtjof Nansen, nor did he ever cherish rancorous feelings in his breast. A quarrel he was ever ready to make up, and this done it was at once and for all forgotten.

The following instance of his school-days shows what his disposition was:—

Fridtjof was in the second class of the primary school. One day a new boy, named Karl, was admitted. Now Fridtjof was the strongest boy in the class, but the newcomer was also a stout-built lad. It happened that they fell out on some occasion or other. Karl was doing something the other did not approve of, whereupon Fridtjof called out, "You've no right to do that."—"Haven't I?" was the reply, and a battle at once ensued. Blood began to flow freely, when the principal appeared on the scene. Taking the two combatants, he locked them up in the class-room. "Sit there, you naughty boys! you ought to be ashamed of yourselves," he said, as he left them in durance vile.

On his return to the class-room a short time afterward, he found the two lads sitting with their arms around each other's neck, reading out of the same book. Henceforth they were bosom friends.

As a boy Nansen possessed singular powers of endurance and hardiness, and could put up with cold, hunger, thirst, or pain to a far greater degree than other boys of his age. But with all this he had a warm heart, sympathizing in the troubles of others, and evincing sincere interest in their welfare,—traits of character of childhood's days that became so strongly developed in Nansen the leader. Side by side with his yearning to achieve exploits there grew up within his breast, under the strict surveillance of his father, the desire of performing good, solid work.

Here may be mentioned another instance, well worthy of notice:—

Fridtjof and his brother went one day to the fair. There were jugglers and cake-stalls and gingerbread, sweets, toys, etc., in abundance. In fine, Christiania fair, coming as it does on the first Tuesday in February, was a very child's paradise, with all its varied attractions. Peasants from the country driving around in their quaint costumes, the townspeople loafing and enjoying themselves, all looking pleased as they made their purchases at the stalls in the marketplace, added to the "fun of the fair."

Fridtjof and his brother Alexander went well furnished with money; for their parents had given them a dime each, while aunt and grandmamma gave them each a quarter apiece. Off the lads started, their faces beaming with joy. On returning home, however, instead of bringing with them sweets and toys, it was seen that they had spent their money in buying tools. Their father was not a little moved at seeing this, and the result was that more money was forthcoming for the lads. But it all went the same way, and was spent in the purchase of tools, with the exception of a nickel that was invested in rye cakes.

More than one boy has on such an occasion remembered his father's and mother's advice not to throw money away on useless things, and has set out with the magnanimous resolve of buying something useful. The difference between them and the Nansen boys is this: the latter not only made good resolutions, but carried them out. It is the act that shows the spirit, and boys who do such things are generally to be met with in later days holding high and responsible positions.

Fridtjof was a diligent boy at school, especially at first, and passed his middle school examination[6] successfully. He worked hard at the natural sciences, which had a special attraction for him. But gradually, as he rose higher in the classes, it was the case with him as it is with others who are destined to perform something exceptional in the world; that is, he preferred to follow out his own ideas—ideas that were not always in accordance with the school plan. His burning thirst after knowledge impelled him to devote his attention to what lay nearest, and thoroughly to investigate whatever was most worthy of note, most wonderful, and most difficult. High aspirations soon make themselves apparent.

The mighty hidden forces of nature had a great attraction for him. He and his friend Karl (who after their fight were inseparable), when Fridtjof was about fifteen, one day got hold of a lot of fireworks. These they mixed up together in a mortar, adding to the compound some "new kinds of fluid" they had bought for their experiment. Nature, however, anticipated them, for a spark happening to fall on the mixture, it burst into flames.

Our two experimentalists thereon seized hold of the mortar and threw it out of the window. It fell on the stones and broke into a thousand pieces, and thus they gained the new experience,—how a new chemical substance should not be compounded. The humorous whim, however, seized them to blacken their hands and faces, and to lie on the floor as if they were dead. And when Alexander entered the room, they made him believe that the explosion had been the cause of it all. Thus, though the experiment had failed, they got some amusement out of its failure.

Although Fridtjof had so many interests outside his actual school studies, he was very diligent in his school work. In 1880 he took his real artium,[7] with twenty-one marks in twelve subjects. In natural science, mathematics, and history he had the best marks, and in the following examination in 1881 he gained the distinction of passing laudabilis præ ceteris.

Though brought up at home very strictly, for his father was extremely particular about the smallest matters, yet his life must have possessed great charm for him, spent as it was in the peaceful quiet of his home at Store Fröen. If on the one hand his father insisted that he should never shirk his duty, but should strictly fulfil it, on the other he never denied him anything that could afford him pleasure.

This is evident from a letter Fridtjof Nansen wrote home during one of his first sojourns among strangers. On writing to his father in 1883 he dwells on the Christmas at home, terms it the highest ideal of happiness and blessedness, dwells on the bright peaceful reminiscences of his childhood and ends with the following description of a Christmas Eve:—

"At last the day dawned,—Christmas Eve. Now impatience was at its height. It was impossible to sit still for one minute; it was absolute necessary to be doing something to get the time to pass, or to occupy one's thoughts either by peeping through the keyhole to try and catch a glimpse of the Christmas-tree with its bags of raisins and almonds, or by rushing out-of-doors and sliding down the hills on a hand-sleigh; or if there were snow enough, we could go out on ski till it was dark. Sometimes it would happen that Einar had to go on an errand into the town, and it was so nice to sit on the saddle at the back of the sleigh, while the sleigh-bells tinkled so merrily, and the stars glittered in the dark sky overhead.

"The long-expected moment arrived at last,—father went in to light up. How my heart thumped and throbbed! Ida was sitting in an armchair in a corner, guessing what would fall to her share; others of the party might be seen to smile in anticipation of some surprise or other of which they had got an inkling—when all at once the doors were thrown wide open, and the dazzling brilliancy of the lights on the Christmas-tree well nigh blinded us. Oh, what a sight it was! For the first few minutes we were literally dumb from joy, could scarcely draw our breath—only a moment afterward to give free vent to our pent-up feelings, like wild things.... Yes—yes—never shall I forget them—never will those Christmas Eves fade from my memory as long as I live."

Reminiscences of a good home, of a good and happy childhood, are the very best things a man can take with him amid the storms and struggles of life; and we may be sure of this,—that on many a day that has been beset with almost insurmountable difficulties, when his powers were almost exhausted, and his heart feeling faint within, the recollection of those early years at Store Fröen has more than once recurred to Nansen's mind.

The peace and comfort of the old home, with all its dear associations, the beloved faces of its inmates—these have passed before his mind's eye, cheering him on in the accomplishment of his last tremendous undertaking.

1. Frognersæteren, a forest-covered hill about six miles from Christiania. Nordmarken, an extensive woodland stretching for miles and miles to the north of Christiania.

2. Statholder, vice-regent. In the early days of the union with Sweden the king had the right of appointing a vice-regent for Norway. The last time the king made use of this prerogative was in 1844, and the right was abrogated in 1872.

3. Foss, waterfall.

4. Ski, Norwegian snowshoes; pronounced shee.

5. Huseby, a farm near Christiania, where the annual ski-match was formerly held.

6. Middle school examination, passed on graduating from the grammar school to the high school.

7. Examen artium, the entrance examination to the university. For real artium the chief topics of examination are sciences, mathematics, and the English language. The best mark in any subject is 1 (excellent), the poorest 6 (bad).

# Chapter II

Youthful Excursions.—Studies.—Goes on a Sealing Expedition to the Arctic Sea.—Hunts Ice-bear.

There is hardly a boy in Christiania or its neighborhood who is fond of sport that does not know Nordmarken, and you may hear many and many a one speak of its lakes, the deafening roar of its cascades, of the mysterious silence of its endless forest tracts, and the refreshing odor of the pine-trees. You may hear, too, how the speckled trout have been lured out of some deep pool, the hare been hunted among the purple mountain ridges, or the capercailzie approached with noiseless footsteps when in early spring the cock bird is wooing his mate; or again, of expeditions on ski over the boundless tracts of snow in the crisp winter air beneath the feathery snowladen trees of the forest.

In the days of Nansen's boyhood it was very different from what it is now. Then the spell of enchantment that ever lies over an unknown and unexplored region brooded over it—a feeling engendered by Asbjörnsen's[1] well-known tales.

It was as if old Asbjörnsen himself, the fairy-tale king, was trudging along rod in hand by the side of some hidden stream—he who alone knew how to find his way through the pathless forest to the dark waters of some remote lake. And it was but once in a while that the most venturesome lads, enticed by the tales he had devoured in that favorite story-book, dared pry into the secrets of that enchanted land. Only a few of the rising generation then had the courage and the hardihood to penetrate into those wilds whence they returned with faces beaming with joy, and with reinvigorated health and strength. But now the whole Norwegian youth do the same thing.

Among the few who in those days ventured there were the Nansen boys. They had the pluck, the hardiness, and yearning after adventure that Nordmarken demanded. They were not afraid of lying out in the forest during a pouring wet summer night, neither were they particular as to whether they had to fast for a day or two.

Fridtjof Nansen was about eleven years old when, in company with his brother Alexander, he paid his first independent visit to it. Two of their friends were living in Sörkedal,[2] so they determined to go and see them—for the forest looked so attractive that they could not resist the temptation. For once they started off without asking leave. They knew their way as far as Bogstad,[3] but after that had to ask the road to Sörkedal. Arriving at their destination, they passed the day in playing games, and in fishing in the river.

But it was not altogether an enjoyable visit, for conscience pricked, and as they set out for home late in the evening, their hearts sank. Their father was a strict disciplinarian, and a thrashing rose up before them, and what was even worse than that, mother might be grieved, and that was something they could not endure to think of.

On reaching home they found its inmates had not gone to bed, though it was late in the night. Of course they had been searching for the truants, and their hearts, which a moment before had been very low down, now jumped up into their throats, for they could see mother coming toward them.

"Is that you, boys?" she asked.

"Now for it," they thought.

"Where have you been?" asked their mother.

Yes, they had been to Sörkedal, and they looked up at her half afraid of what would happen next. Then they saw that her eyes were filled with tears.

"You are strange boys!" she murmured; and that was all she said. But those words made the hearts of the young culprits turn cold and hot by turns, and they there and then registered a vow that they would never do anything again to cause mother pain, but would always try to please her—a resolution they kept, as far as was possible, their whole lives through.

Subsequently they had leave given them to go to Sörkedal, and wherever else they wanted. But they had to go on their own responsibility, and look out for themselves as best they could. But Fridtjof never forgot the lesson he had learned on that first expedition to Nordmarken. Who can tell whether his mother's tearful face, and her gentle words, "You are strange boys!" have not appeared to him in wakeful hours, and been the means of preventing many a venturesome deed being rashly undertaken, many a headstrong idea from becoming defiant.

This at all events is certain,—Nansen when a man always knew how to turn aside in a spirit of self-denial when the boundary line between prudence and rashness had been reached. And for this it may be safely said he had to thank his father and mother.

---

Those who are in the habit of going about in forests are pretty sure to meet with some wonderful old fellow who knows where the best fish lie in the river, and the favorite haunts of game in the woods. Such a one was an old man named Ola Knub, whose acquaintance Nansen made in the Nordmarken forest. His wife used to come to Store Fröen with baskets of huckleberries, strawberries, cranberries, etc., and it was through her Fridtjof got to know him. Often they would set off on an expedition, rod in hand, and coffee kettle on their back, and be away for days together. They would fish for trout from early morning till late at night, sleeping on a plank bed in some wood-cutter's hut, after partaking of a supper of trout broiled in the ashes, and black coffee.

Toward the end of May, when the birch and the oak began to bud, and the timber floats had gone down the river, they would start on such an expedition, taking with them a goodly supply of bread and butter, and perhaps the stump of a sausage.

It took them generally quite five hours to reach their destination, but once arrived there they would immediately set to work with rod and line, and fish up to midnight, when they would crawl into some charcoal-burner's hut for a few hours' sleep, or as was often the case, sleep out in the open, resting their backs against a tree, and then at daybreak would be off again, to the river. For time was precious, and they had to make the best use they could of the hours between Saturday evening and Monday morning, when they must be in school.

When autumn set in, and hare-hunting began, they would often be on foot for twenty-four hours together without any food at all. As the boys grew older, they would follow the chase in winter on ski, often, indeed, almost to the detriment of their health. Once when they had been hare-hunting for a whole fortnight, they found their provision-bag was empty, and as they would not touch the hares they had killed, they had to subsist as best they could on potatoes only.

In this way Fridtjof grew up to be exceptionally hardy. When, as it often happened, his companions got worn out, he would suggest their going to some spot a long distance off. It seemed to be a special point of honor with him to bid defiance to fatigue. On one occasion, after one of these winter excursions to Nordmarken, he set off alone without any provisions in his knapsack to a place twenty-five kilometres (fifteen and a half miles) distant, for none of his companions dared accompany him. On arriving at the place where he was bound, he almost ate its inmates out of house and home.

On another occasion, on a long expedition on ski with some of his comrades, all of whom had brought a plentiful supply of food with them in their knapsacks, Fridtjof had nothing. When they halted to take some necessary refreshment, he unbuttoned his jacket and pulled out some pancakes from his pocket, quite warm from the heat of his body. "Here, you fellows," he said, "won't you have some pancakes?" But pancakes, his friends thought, might be nice things in general, yet pancakes kept hot in that way were not appetizing, and so they refused his proffered hospitality.

"You are a lot of geese! there's jam on them too," he said, as he eagerly devoured the lot.

Even as a boy Fridtjof was impressed with the idea that hardiness and powers of endurance were qualifications absolutely essential for the life he was bent on leading; so he made it his great aim to be able to bear everything, and to require as little as was possible.

If there were things others found impracticable, he would at once set to work and attempt them. And when once he had taken a matter in hand, he would never rest till he had gone through with it, even though his life might be at stake. For instance, he and his brother once set out to climb the Svartdal's peak in Jotunheim.[4] People usually made the ascent from the rear side of the mountain; but this was not difficult enough for him. He would climb it from the front, a route no one had ever attempted; and he did it.

Up under Svartdal's peak there was a glacier that they must cross, bounded on its farther side by a precipice extending perpendicularly down into the valley below. His brother relates, "I had turned giddy, so Fridtjof let me have his staff. Then he set off over the ice; but instead of going with the utmost caution, advancing foot by foot at a time, as he now would do, off went my brother as hard as he could—his foot slipped, and he commenced to slide down the glacier. I saw that he turned pale, for in a few seconds more he would be hurled over the abyss, and be crushed to pieces on the rocks below. He saw his danger, however, just in the nick of time, and managed to arrest his progress by digging his heels into the snow. Never shall I forget that moment; neither shall I forget when we arrived at the tourist's cabin how he borrowed a pair of trousers belonging to the club's corpulent secretary—for they completely swallowed him up. His own garment, be it stated, had lost an essential part by the excessive friction caused by his slide down the glacier."

Such were the foolhardy exploits Fridtjof would indulge in as a boy; but when he arrived at manhood he would never risk his life in any undertaking that was not worth a life's venture.

---

When nineteen he entered the university, and in the following year passed his second examination;[5] and now arose the question what was he to be? As yet the idea of the future career which has rendered his name famous had not occurred to his mind, so we see him hesitating over which of the many roads that lay before him to adopt. He applied to have his name put down for admission as cadet in the military school, but quickly withdrew the application. Next he began the study of medicine, after which all his time was devoted to a special study of zoölogy. In 1882 he sought the advice of Professor Collet as to the best method of following up this branch of science, and the professor's reply was that he had better go on a sealing-expedition to the Arctic seas. Nansen took a week to reflect on this advice before finally deciding; and on March 11 we see him on board the sealer Viking, steering out of Arendal harbor to the Arctic ocean—the ocean that subsequently was to mark an epoch in his life, and become the scene of his memorable exploit.

*Picture: Nansen at nineteen*

It was with wondrously mixed feelings that he turned his gaze toward the north as he stood on the deck that March morning. Behind him lay the beloved home of his childhood and youth. The first rays of the rising sun were shining over the silent forests whither the woodcock and other birds of passage would soon be journeying from southern climes, and the capercailzie beginning his amorous manœuvres on the sombre pine tops, while the whole woodland would speedily be flooded with the songs of its feathered denizens.

And there before him was the sea, the wondrous sea, where he would behold wrecked vessels drifting along in the raging tempest, with flocks of stormy petrels in attendance—and beyond, the Polar sea, that fairy region, was pictured in his dreams. Yes, he could see it in his spirit—could see the mighty icebergs, with their crests sparkling in the sunlight in thousands of varied forms and hues, and between these the boundless tracts of ice extending as far as the eye could reach in one level unbroken plain. When this dream became reality, how did he meet it?

Flat, drifting floes of ice, rocked up and down in the blue-green sea, alike in sunshine and in fog, in storm and calm. One monotonous infinity of ice to struggle through, floe after floe rising up like white-clad ghosts from the murky sea, gliding by with a soughing, rippling murmur to vanish from sight, or to dash against the ship's sides till masts and hull quivered; and then when morning broke, a faint, mysterious light, a hollow murmur in the air, like the roar of distant surge, far away to the north.

This was the Arctic sea! this the drift ice! They were soon in the midst of it. The sea-gulls circled about, and the snow-bunting whirled around the floes of ice on which the new-fallen snow lay and glittered.

A gale set in; then it blew a hurricane; and the Viking groaned like a wounded whale, quivering as if in the agonies of death from the fierce blows on her sides. At last they approached the scene of their exertions, and the excitement of the impending chase for seals drove out every other feeling from the mind, and every one was wondering "were there many seals this year? would the weather be propitious?"

One forenoon "a sail to leeward" was reported by the man in the crow's-nest, and all hands were called up on deck, every stitch of canvas spread, and all the available steam-power used to overtake the stranger.

There were two ships; one of them being Nordenskjöld's famous Vega, now converted into a sealer. Nansen took his hat off to her; and it may well be that this strange encounter imbued his mind with a yearning to accomplish some exploit of a similar perilous nature and world-wide renown as that of the famed Vega expedition. It is a significant fact that the Vega was the first ship Nansen met with in the Arctic sea—a fact that forces itself upon the mind with all the might of a historic moment, with all the fateful force of destiny. It addresses us like one of those many accidental occurrences that seem as if they had a purpose—occurrences that every man who is on the alert and mindful of his future career will meet once at least if not oftener on his journey through life. Such things are beyond our finite comprehension. Some people may term them "the finger of God," others the new, higher, unknown laws of nature; it may be these names signify but one and the same thing.

That year the Viking did not meet with great success among the seals, for the season was rather too advanced by the time she reached the sealing-grounds. But all the more did Nansen get to learn about the Arctic sea; and of the immense waste of waters of that free, lonely ocean, his inmost being drank in refreshing draughts.

On May 2, Spitzbergen was sighted, and on the 25th they were off the coast of Iceland, where Nansen for a while planted his foot once more on firm land. But their stay there was short, and soon they were off to sea again, and in among the seals. And now the continual report of guns sounded all around; the crew singing and shouting; flaying seals and boiling the blubber—a life forsooth of busy activity.

Toward the end of June the Viking got frozen in off the East Greenland coast, where she lay imprisoned a whole month, unfortunately during the best of the sealing season; a loss, indeed, to the owners, but a gain for Nansen, who now for the first time in his life got his full enjoyment in the chase of the polar bear.

During all these days of their imprisonment in the ice there was one incessant chase after bears,—looking out for bears from the crow's-nest, racing after bears over the ice, resulting in loss of life to a goodly number of those huge denizens of the Polar regions.

"Bear on the weather bow!" "Bear to leeward! all hands turn out!" were the cries from morning till night; and many a time did Nansen jump up from his berth but half dressed, and away over the ice to get a shot.

Toward evening one day in July Nansen was sitting up in the crow's-nest, making a sketch of the Greenland coast. On deck one of the crew, nicknamed Balloon, was keeping watch, and just as our artist was engrossed with his pencil, he heard Balloon shouting at the top of his voice, "Bear ahead!" In an instant Nansen sprang up, threw his painting-materials down on the deck below, quickly following the same himself down the rigging. But alas! by the time he had reached the deck and seized his rifle, the bear had disappeared.

"A pretty sort of fellow to sit up in the crow's-nest and not see a bear squatting just in front of the bows!" said the captain tauntingly.

But a day or two afterward Nansen fully retrieved his reputation. It was his last bear-hunt on the expedition, and this is what occurred:—

He and the captain and one of the sailors set out after a monstrous bear. The beast, however, was shy, and beat a speedy retreat. All three sprang after it. But as Nansen was jumping over an open place in the ice, he fell plump into the sea. His first thought on finding himself in the water was his rifle, which he flung upon the ice. But it slipped off again into the water, so Nansen had to dive after it. Next time he managed to throw it some distance across the ice, and then clambered up himself, of course wet through to the skin. But his cartridges, which were water-tight ones, were all right, and soon he rejoined his companions in pursuit, and outstripped them. In a little while he saw the bear making for a hummock, and made straight for him; on coming up to closer quarters the beast turned sharp round and dropped into the water, but not before Nansen was able to put a bullet into him. On reaching the edge of the ice, he could see no trace of the animal. Yes—there was something white yonder, a little below the surface, for the bear had dived. Presently he saw the animal pop its head up just in front of him, and a moment after its paws were on the edge of the floe, on which, with a fierce and angry growl, the huge beast managed to drag himself up. Nansen now fired again, and had the satisfaction of seeing the bear drop back dead into the water, where he had to hold it by the ears to prevent it sinking, till his companions came up, when they were able to haul it up on the ice.

The captain now bade Nansen return to the ship as quickly as he could to change his clothes; but on his road thither he met with some others of the crew in pursuit of a couple of bears. The temptation was too strong for him, so he joined them. He was fortunate enough to shoot one of the bears that they had wounded, and then started after bear number two, which was leisurely devouring the carcass of a seal some little distance off. On coming up with it he fired. The bear reeled and fell backwards into the water, but speedily coming up again, made off for a large hummock, under cover of which it hoped to be able to sneak off.

But Nansen was not far behind. It was an exciting chase. First over a wide space of open water, then across some firm ice; the bear dashed along for dear life, and now the iron muscles, hardened by his exploits on the Huseby hills and his Nordmarken experiences, stood his pursuer in good stead. Following on the blood-stained track, he ran as fast as his legs could carry him. Now the bear, now Nansen, seemed to be getting the advantage. Whenever a broad opening in the ice or a pool of clear water came in their way, they swam across it; bear first, Nansen a good second—and so it went on mile after mile. Presently, however, Nansen thought his competitor in the race began to slacken speed, and to turn and twist in his course, as if seeking for some friendly shelter; and coming up within a reasonable distance he gave him two bullets, one lodging in the chest, the other behind the ear, when to his great joy the bear lay dead at his feet. Nansen at once set to work to skin the brute with a penknife—rather a tedious operation with such an instrument. Presently one of the sailors came up, and off they started for the ship with the skin, on their road meeting a man whom the captain had thoughtfully despatched with a supply of bread and meat, without which, indeed, as is well known, a hero, especially when ravenously hungry, is a nobody.

In all, nineteen bears were bagged during this time.

Soon after this bear-hunt the Viking set out for home, and great was the joy of all on board when the coast of "old Norway," with its lofty mountain ridges, was seen towering up over the sea. This expedition of the Viking was termed by the sailors, "Nansen's cruise,"—an exceptional reminiscence, a monolith in the midst of the ice!

"Ay, he was a chap after bears!" said one of the sailors afterward; "just as much under the water as over it, when he was after bears. I told him that he was going to injure his health that way; but he only laughed, and pointing to his woollen jersey said, 'I do not feel cold.'"

To Fridtjof Nansen this Arctic expedition became the turning-point of his life. The dream of the mighty ocean never left him; it was ever before his eyes with all its inexplicable riddles.

Here was something to do—something that people called impossible. He would test it. Some years, however, must elapse before that dream should become reality. Nansen must first be a man. Everything that tended to retard his progress must be removed or shattered to pieces—all that would promote it, improved upon and set in order.

---

1. P. C. Asbjörnsen (pron. Asbyurnsen) together with Jörgen (pron. Yurgen) Moe collected the popular and fairy tales of Norway.
2. Sörkedal, a valley about eight miles to the north of Christiania.
3. Bogstad, a baronial manor about five miles north of Christiania.
4. Jotunheim, the giant's world, a group of mountains in the centre of southern Norway.
5. Second examination, graduating as a bachelor of arts.

# Chapter III

FRIDTJOF NANSEN ACCEPTS A POSITION IN THE BERGEN MUSEUM.—
CROSSES THE MOUNTAINS IN THE WINTER.—PREPARES HIMSELF FOR THE
DOCTOR'S DEGREE.

The very same day that Nansen set foot on land after his return from this expedition he was offered the Conservatorship of the Bergen[1] Museum by Professor Collett. Old Danielsen, the chief physician, a man of iron capacity for work, and who had attained great renown in his profession, wanted to place a new man in charge. Nansen promptly accepted the offer, but asked first to be allowed to visit a sister in Denmark. But a telegram from Danielsen, "Nansen must come at once," compelled him, though with no little regret, to give up his projected visit.

The meeting of these two men was as if two clouds heavily laden with electricity had come in contact, producing a spark that blazed over the northern sky. That spark resulted in the famous Greenland expedition.

Danielsen was one of those who held that a youth possessed of health, strength, and good abilities should be able to unravel almost anything and everything in this world, and in Fridtjof Nansen he found such an one. So these two worked together assiduously; for both were alike enthusiastic in the cause of science, both possessed the same strong faith in its advancement. And Danielsen, the clear-headed scientist, after being associated with his colleague for some few years, entertained such firm confidence in his powers and capabilities, that a short time before the expedition to the North Pole set out, he wrote in a letter:—

"Fridtjof Nansen will as surely return crowned with success from the North Pole as it is I who am writing these lines—such is an old man's prophecy!"

The old scientist, who felt his end was drawing near, sent him before his death an anticipatory letter of greeting when the expedition should happily be over.

Nansen devoted himself to the study of science with the same indomitable energy that characterized all of his achievements.

Hour by hour he would sit over his microscope, month after month devote himself to the pursuit of knowledge. Yet every now and then, when he felt he must go out to get some fresh air, he would buckle on his ski, and dash along over the mountain or through the forest till the snow spurted up in clouds behind him. Thus he spent several years in Bergen.

But one fine day, chancing to read in the papers that Nordenskjöld had returned from his expedition to Greenland, and had said that the interior of the country was a boundless plain of ice and snow, it flashed on his mind that here was a field of work for him. Yes—he would cross Greenland on ski! and he at once set to work to prepare a plan for the expedition. But such an adventurous task, in which life would be at stake, must not be undertaken till he himself had become a proficient in that branch of science which he had selected as his special study. So he remains yet some more years in Bergen, after which he spends twelve months in Naples, working hard at the subjects in which he subsequently took his doctor's degree in 1888.

Those years of expectation in Bergen were busy years. Every now and then he would become homesick. In winter time he would go by the railway from Bergen to Voss,[2] thence on ski over the mountains to Christiania, down the Stalheim road,[3] with its sinuous twists and bends, on through Nærödal, noted for its earth slips, on by the swift Lerdals river fretting and fuming on one side, and a perpendicular mountain wall on the other. And here he would sit to rest in that narrow gorge where avalanches are of constant occurrence. Let them come! he must rest awhile and eat. A solitary wayfarer hurries by on his sleigh as fast as his horse will go. "Take care!" shouts the traveller as he passes by; and Nansen looks up, gathers his things together, and proceeds on his journey through the valley. It was Sauekilen, the most dangerous spot in Lerdals, where he was resting. Then the night falls, the moon shines brightly overhead, and the creaking sound of his footsteps follows him over the desert waste, and his dark-blue shadow stays close beside him. And he, the man possessed of ineffable pride and indomitable resolution, feels how utterly insignificant he is in that lonely wilderness of snow—naught but an insect under the powerful microscope of the starlit sky, for the far-seeing eye of the Almighty is piercing through his inmost soul. Here it avails not to seek to hide aught from that gaze. So he pours out his thoughts to Him who alone has the right to search them. That midnight pilgrimage over the snowy waste was like a divine service on ski; and it was as an invigorated man, weary though he was in body, that he knocked at the door of a peasant's cabin, while its astonished inmates looked out in amazement, and the old housewife cried out, "Nay! in Jesus' name, are there folk on the fjeld[4] so late in the night? Nay! is it you? Suppose you are always so late on the road!"

Even still more arduous was the return journey that same winter. The people in the last house on the eastern side of the mountain, in bidding him "God speed," entreat him to go cautiously, for the road over the fjeld is well nigh impassable in winter, they say. Not a man in the whole district would follow him, they add. Nansen promises them to be very careful, as he sets off in the moonlight at three o'clock in the morning. Soon he reaches the wild desert, and the glittering snow blushes like a golden sea in the beams of the rising sun. Presently he reaches Myrstölen.[5] The houseman is away from home, and the women-folk moan and weep on learning the road he means to take. On resuming his journey he shortly comes to a cross-road. Shall it be Aurland or Vosse skavlen?[6] He chooses the latter route across the snow plateau, for it is the path the wild reindeer follow. On he skims over the crisp surface enveloped in the cloud of snow-dust his ski stir up, for the wind is behind him. But now he loses his way, falls down among the clefts and fissures, toils along step by step, and at last has to turn back and retrace his steps. There ought to be a sæter[7] somewhere about there, but it seems as if it had been spirited away. A pitchy darkness sets in; for the stars have disappeared one by one, and the night is of a coal-black hue, and Fridtjof has to make his bed on the snow-covered plateau, under the protecting shelter of a bowlder, his faithful dog by his side, his knapsack for a pillow, while the night wind howls over the waste.

Again, at three in the morning, he resumes his journey, only again to lose his way, and burying himself in the snow, determines to wait for daybreak. Dawn came over the mountain-tops in a sea of rosy light, while the dark shadows of night fled to their hiding-places in the deep valleys below—a proclamation of eternity, where nature was the preacher and nature the listener, the voice of God speaking to himself.

At broad daylight he sees Vosse skavlen close at hand, and thither he drags his weary, stiffened limbs; but on reaching the summit he drinks "skaal[8] to the fjeld," a frozen orange, the last he has, being his beverage. Before the sun sets again, Fridtjof has crossed that mountain height, as King Sverre[9] did of yore—an achievement performed by those two alone!

---

Fridtjof Nansen's father died in 1885, and it was largely consideration for his aged parent's failing health during the last few years that delayed Nansen's setting out on his Greenland expedition. The letters that passed between father and son during this period strikingly evince the tender relationship existing between them. On receipt of the tidings of his father's last illness he hurried off at a moment's notice, never resting on his long homeward journey, inexpressibly grieved at arriving too late to see him alive.

Then, after a year's sojourn in Naples, where he met the genial and energetic Professor Dohrn, the founder of the biological station[10] in that city, having no further ties to hinder him, he enters heart and soul into the tasks he has set himself to accomplish,—to take his degree as doctor of philosophy, and to make preparation for his expedition to Greenland, both of which tasks he accomplished in the same year with credit. For he not only made himself a name as a profound researcher in the realms of science, but at the same time equipped an expedition that was soon destined to excite universal attention, not in the north alone, but throughout the length and breadth of Europe.

1. Bergen, the metropolis of western Norway, the second largest city in Norway

2. Voss, a country district of western Norway, connected with Bergen by railway.

3. Stalheim road, a piece of road winding in a slow decline down a steep hill, famous for the beauty of its scenery and the engineering skill with which it has been built. Nærödal and Lerdals river must be passed on the way from Bergen to Christiania.

4. Fjeld (pron. fyell), mountain.

5. Myrstölen, the last house on the eastern side of the mountain inhabited the whole year through.

6. Aurland and Vosse skavlen, alternative routes across the mountains from Christiania to Bergen.

7. Sæter, mountain hut, used by graziers during the summer months.

8. Skaal, your health.

9. King Sverre, King of Norway 1177 to 1202.

10. An institution where animal life is studied.

# Chapter IV

Nansen Meets Nordenskjöld.[1]—Preparations for the Greenland Expedition.—Nansen's Followers on the Expedition.—Starting on the Expedition.—Drifting on an Ice-floe.—Landing on East Coast of Greenland.

Nansen had an arduous task before him in the spring of 1888, one that demanded all his strength and energy, for he would take his doctor's degree, and make preparations for his expedition to Greenland.

He had already, in the autumn of 1887, made up his mind to accomplish both these things. In November of that year, accordingly, he went to Stockholm to confer with Nordenskjöld. Professor Brögger, who introduced him to that gentleman, gives the following account of the interview:—

"On Thursday, Nov. 3, as I was sitting in my study in the Mineralogical Institute, my messenger came in and said a Norwegian had been inquiring for me. He had left no card, neither had he given his name. Doubtless, I thought, it was some one who wanted help out of a difficulty.

"'What was he like?' I inquired.

"'Tall and fair,' replied the messenger.

"'Was he dressed decently?' I asked.

"'He hadn't an overcoat on.' This with a significant smile, as he added, 'Looked for all the world like a seafaring man—or a tramp.'

"'Humph!' I muttered to myself; 'sailor with no overcoat! Very likely thinks I'm going to give him one—yes, I think I understand.'

"Later on in the afternoon Wille[2] came in. 'Have you seen Nansen?' he said.

"'Nansen?' I replied. 'Was that sailor fellow without an overcoat Nansen?'

"'Without an overcoat! Why, he means to cross over the inland ice of Greenland;' and out went Wille—he was in a hurry.

"Presently entered Professor Lecke with the same question, 'Have you seen Nansen? Isn't he a fine fellow? such a lot of interesting discoveries he told me of, and then his researches into the nervous system—a grand fellow!' and off went Lecke.

"But before long the man himself entered the room. Tall, upright, broad-shouldered, strongly built, though slim and very youthful looking, with his shock of hair brushed off his well-developed forehead. Coming toward me and holding out his hand, he introduced himself by name, while a pleasing smile played over his face.

"'And you mean to cross over Greenland?' I asked.

"'Yes; I've been thinking of it,' was the reply.

"I looked him in the face, as he stood before me with an air of conscious self-reliance about him. With every word he spoke he seemed to grow on me; and this plan of his to cross over Greenland on ski from the east coast, which but a moment ago I had looked on as a madman's idea, during our conversation gradually grew on me, till it seemed to be the most natural thing in the world; and all at once it flashed on my mind, 'And he'll do it, too, as sure as ever we are sitting here talking about it.'

"He, whose name but two hours ago I had not known, became in those few minutes (and it all came about so naturally) as if he were an old acquaintance, and I felt I should be proud and fortunate indeed to have him for my friend my whole life through.

"'We will go and see Nordenskjöld at once,' I said, rising up. And we went.

"With his strange attire,—he was dressed in a tight-fitting, dark-blue blouse or coatee, a kind of knitted jacket,—he was, as may be supposed, stared at in Drottning-gatan. Some people, indeed, took him for an acrobat or tight-rope dancer."

Nordenskjöld, "old Nor" as he was often termed, was in his laboratory, and looked up sharply as his two visitors entered the room, for he was, as ever, "busy."

The professor saluted, and introduced his companion, "Conservator Nansen from Bergen, who purposes to cross over the inland ice of Greenland."

"The deuce he does!" muttered "old Nor," staring with all his eyes at the fair-haired young viking.

"And would like to confer with you about it," continued the professor.

"Quite welcome; and so Herr Nansen thinks of crossing over Greenland?"

"Yes; such was his intention." Thereon, without further ado, he sketched out his projected plan, to which "old Nor" listened with great attention, shaking his head every now and then, as if rather sceptical about it, but evidently getting more and more interested as he proceeded.

As Nansen and Professor Brögger were sitting in the latter's house that evening, a knock was heard at the door, and who should come in but "old Nor" himself—a convincing proof to Brögger that the old man entertained a favorable idea of the proposed plan. And many a valuable hint did the young ice-bear get from the old one, as they sat opposite each other—the man of the past and the coming man of the present—quietly conversing together that evening.

Now Nansen sets off for home in order to prepare for the arduous task of the ensuing spring. In December, 1887, he is in Bergen again, and at the end of January he travels on ski from Hardanger to Kongsberg, thence by rail to Christiania.

In March we see him once more in Bergen, giving lectures in order to awaken public interest in Greenland; now sleeping out on the top of Blaamand,[3] a mountain near Bergen, in a sleeping-bag, to test its efficiency; now standing on the cathedra in the university auditorium to claim his right to the degree of doctor of philosophy, which on April 28 was honorably awarded him; and on May 2 he sets out for Copenhagen, en route for Greenland. For unhappily it was the case in Norway in 1888 that Norwegian exploits must be carried out with Danish help. In vain had he sought for assistance from the regents of the university. They recommended the matter to the government, but the government had no 5,000 kroner[4] ($1,350) to throw away on such an enterprise,—the enterprise of a madman, as most people termed it.

Yet when that enterprise had been carried to a successful issue, and that same lunatic had become a great man and asked the government and the storthing[5] for a grant of 200,000 kroner ($54,000) for his second mad expedition, his request was promptly granted. A new Norway had grown up meanwhile, a new national spirit had forced its way into existence, a living testimony to the power of the Nansen expedition.

As stated above, Nansen had to go to Denmark for the 5,000 kroner; and it was the wealthy merchant, Augustin Gamel, who placed that amount at his disposal. Still, certain is it, had not that sum of money been forthcoming as it was, Fridtjof Nansen would have plucked himself bare to the last feather in order to carry out his undertaking.

But what was there to be gained from an expedition to Greenland worth the risking of human life,—for a life-risk it unquestionably would be,—to say nothing of the cost thereof? What was there to be learned from the ice?

The question is soon answered.

The island of Greenland,—for it is now well ascertained that it is an island, and that the largest in the world,—this Sahara of the North, contains within its ice-plains the key to the history of the human race. For it is the largest homogeneous relic we possess of the glacial age. Such as Greenland now is, so large tracts of the world have been; and, what is of more interest to us, so has the whole of the north been. It is this mighty ice-realm that has caused a large proportion of the earth's surface to assume its present appearance. The lowlands of Mid-Germany and Denmark have been scoured and transported thither from the rocks of Norway and Sweden. The Swedish rock at Lützen in Saxony is Swedish granite that the ice has carried with it. And the small glaciers still left in Norway, such as the Folgefond, Jostedalsbræ, Svartis,[6] etc., are merely "calves" of that ancient, stupendous mass of ice that time and heat have transported, even though it once lay more than a thousand metres in thickness over widely extended plains.

To investigate, therefore, the inland ice of Greenland is, in a word, to investigate the great glacial age; and one may learn from such a study many a lesson explanatory of our earth's appearance at the present day, and ascertain what could exist, and what could not, under such conditions.

We know now that, during the glacial age, human beings lived on this earth, even close up to this gigantic glacier, that subsequently destroyed all life on its course. It may be safely asserted that the struggle with the ice, and with the variations of climate, have been important factors in making the human race what it will eventually be, the lords of nature.

The Esquimaux in their deerskin dress, the aborigines of Australia, the pigmy tribes of Africa's primeval forests, are a living testimony of the tenacious powers of the soul and body of mankind,—civilization's trusty outposts. An Esquimau living on blubber under fifty degrees of cold is just as much a man of achievement in this work-a-day world as an Edison, who, with every comfort at his disposal, forces nature to disclose her hidden marvels. But he who, born in the midst of civilization, and who forces his way to an outpost farther advanced than any mankind has yet attained, is greater, perhaps, than either, especially when in his struggle for existence he wrests from nature her inmost secrets.

This was the kernel of Nansen's exploits—his first and his last.

---

Nansen was fully alive to the fact that his enterprise would involve human life; and he formed his plans in such wise that he would either attain his object or perish in the attempt. He would make the dangerous, uninhabited coast of East Greenland his starting-point as one which presented no enticement for retracing his steps. He would force his way onward. The instinct of self-preservation should impel him toward the west—the greater his advance in that direction the greater his hopes. Behind him naught but death; before him, life!

But he must have followers! Where were men to be found to risk their lives on such a venture? to form one of a madman's retinue? And not only that, he must have men with him who, like himself, were well versed in all manly sports, especially in running on ski; men hard as iron, as he was; men who, like himself, were unencumbered with family ties. Where were such to be found? He sought long and diligently, and he found them.

There was a man named Sverdrup—Otto Sverdrup. Yes, we all of us know him now! But then he was an unknown Nordland youth, inured to hardship on sea and land, an excellent sailor, a skilful ski-runner, firm of purpose; one to whom fatigue was a stranger, physically strong and able in emergency, unyielding as a rod of iron, firm as a rock. A man chary of words in fine weather, but eloquent in storm: possessed, too, of a courage that lay so deep that it needed almost a peril involving life to arouse it. Yet, when the pinch came Sverdrup was in his element. Then would his light blue eyes assume a darker hue, and a smile creep over his hard-set features; then he would resemble a hawk that sits on a perch with ruffled feathers, bidding defiance to every one who approaches it, but which, when danger draws nigh, flaps its pinions, and soars aloft in ever widening circles, increasing with the force of the tempest, borne along by the storm.

This man accompanied him.

*Picture: Otto Sverdrup*

Number two was Lieutenant, now Captain, Olaf Dietrichson. He, too, hailed from the north. A man who loved a life in the open air, a master in all manly exploits, elastic as a steel spring, a proficient on ski, and a sportsman in heart and soul. And added to this, a man possessed of great knowledge in those matters especially that were needed in an expedition like the present. He, too, was enrolled among the number. Number three was also from Nordland, from Sverdrup's neighborhood, who recommended him. His name was Kristian Kristiansen Trana—a handy and reliable youth.

These three were all Nordlanders. But Nansen had a great desire to have a couple of Fjeld-Finns with him, for he considered that, inured as they were to ice and snow, their presence would be of great service to him. They came from Karasjok.[7] The one a fine young fellow, more Qvæn[8] than Lapp; the other a little squalid-looking, dark-haired, pink-eyed Fjeld-Finn. The name of the first was Balto; of the other, Ravna. These two children of the mountains came to Christiania looking dreadfully perplexed, with little of the heroic about them. For they had agreed to accompany the expedition principally for the sake of the good pay, and now learned for the first time that their lives might be endangered. Nansen, however, managed to instil a little confidence into them, and as was subsequently proved, they turned out to be useful and reliable members of the expedition. Old Ravna, who was forty-five, was a married man,—a fact Nansen did not know when he engaged him,—and was possessed of great physical strength and powers of endurance.

Nansen now had the lives of five persons beside his own on his conscience. He would, therefore, make his equipment in such manner that he should have nothing to reproach himself with in case anything went wrong, a work that he conscientiously and carefully carried out. There was not a single article or implement that was not scientifically and practically discussed and tested, measured and weighed, before they set out. Hand-sleighs and ski, boats and tent, cooking-utensils, sleeping-bags, shoes and clothes, food and drink, all were of the best kind; plenty of everything, but nothing superfluous—light, yet strong, nourishing and strengthening. Everything, in fact, was well thought over, and as was subsequently proved, the mistakes that did occur were few and trifling.

Nansen made most of the implements with his own hands, and nothing came to pieces during the whole expedition saving a boat plank that was crushed by the ice.

But one thing Nansen omitted to take with him, and that was a supply of spirituous liquor. It did not exist in his dictionary of sport. For he had long entertained the opinion—an opinion very generally held by the youth of Norway at the present day—that strong drink is a foe to manly exploit, sapping and undermining man's physical and mental powers. In former days, indeed, in Norway, as elsewhere, it was considered manly to drink, but now the drinker is looked down on with a pity akin to contempt.

Thus equipped, these six venturesome men set out on their way; first by steamer to Iceland, thence by the Jason, a sealer, Captain Jacobsen its commander, who, as opportunity should offer, was to set them ashore on the east coast of Greenland. And here, after struggling for a month with the ice, they finally arrived, on July 19, so near to the Sermilik Fjord that Nansen determined to leave the Jason and make his way across the ice to land. The whole ship's crew were on deck to bid them farewell. Nansen was in command of one of the two boats, and when he gave the word "set off," they shot off from the ship's side, while the Jason's two guns and a spontaneous hurrah from sixty-four stalwart sailors' throats resounded far and wide over the sea. As the boats worked their way into the ice, the Jason changed her course, and ere long our six travellers watched the Norwegian flag, waving like a distant tongue of fire, gradually fade from sight and disappear among the mist and fog.

These six men set out on their arduous journey with all the indomitable fearlessness and disregard of danger that youth inspires,—qualifications that would speedily be called into requisition.

Before many hours of toiling in the ice, the rain came down in torrents, and the current drove them with irresistible force away from the land, while ice-floes kept striking against their boats' sides, threatening to crush or capsize them. A plank, indeed, in Nansen's boat was broken by the concussion, and had to be instantly repaired, the rain meanwhile pouring down a perfect deluge. They determined, therefore, to drag the boats upon an ice-floe, and to pitch their tent on it; and having done this they got into their sleeping-bags, the deafening war of the raging storm in their ears. The two Fjeld-Lapps, however, thinking their end was drawing near, sat with a dejected air gazing in silence out over the sea.

*Picture: Camp on the drift-ice*

Far away in the distance the roar of the surge dashing against the edge of the ice could be heard, while the steadily increasing swell portended an approaching tempest.

Next morning, July 20, Nansen was awakened by a violent concussion. The ice-floe on which they were was rent asunder, and the current was rapidly drifting them out toward the open sea. The roar of the surge increased; the waves broke over the ice-floe on all sides. Balto and Ravna lay crouching beneath a tarpaulin reading the New Testament in Lappish, while the tears trickled down their cheeks; but out on the floe Dietrichson and Kristiansen were making jokes as every fresh wave dashed over them. Sverdrup was standing with hands folded behind his back, chewing his quid, his eyes directed towards the sea, as if in expectation.

They are but a few hundred metres distant from the open sea, and soon will have to take to the boats, or be washed off the floe. The swell is so heavy that the floe ducks up and down like a boat in the trough of the sea. So the order is given, "All hands turn in," for all their strength will be needed, in the fierce struggle they will shortly have to encounter. So they sleep on the very brink of death, the roar of the storm their lullaby—Ravna and Balto in one of the boats, Nansen and the others in the tent, where the water pours in and out.

But there is one outside, on the floe. It is his watch. Hour by hour he walks up and down, his hands behind his back. It is Sverdrup. Every now and then he stands still, turns his sharp, thin face with the sea-blue eyes towards the breakers, and then once more resumes his walk.

The storm is raging outside, and the surge is dashing over the ice. He goes to the boat where Ravna and Balto lie sleeping, and lays hold of it, lest it should be swept away by the backwash. Then he goes to the tent, undoes a hook, and again stands gazing over the sea; then turns round, and resumes his walk as before.

Their floe is now at the extreme edge of the ice, close to the open sea. A huge crag of ice rises up like some white-clad threatening monster, and the surf dashes furiously over the floe. Again the man on the watch arrests his steps; he undoes another hook in the tent. Matters are at their worst! He must arouse his comrades! He is about to do so when he turns once more and gazes seaward. He becomes aware of a new and strange motion in the floe beneath him. Its course is suddenly changed; it is speeding swiftly away from the open sea—inward, ever inward toward calm water, toward life, toward safety. And as that bronze-faced man stands there, a strange and serious look passes over his features. For that has occurred,—that wondrous thing that he and many another sailor has often experienced,—salvation from death without the mediation of human agency. That moment was for him what the stormy night on the Hardanger waste was to Nansen. It was like divine service! It was as if some invisible hand had steered the floe, he said afterwards to Nansen. So he rolled his quid round into the other cheek, stuck his hands in his pockets; and hour after hour, till late in the morning, the steps of that iron-hearted man on the watch might be heard pacing to and fro.

When Nansen awoke, the floe was in safe shelter.

Still for another week they kept drifting southward, the glaciers and mountain ridges one after another disappearing from view—a weary, comfortless time. Then, toward midnight on July 28, when it was Sverdrup's watch again, he thought he could hear the sound of breakers in the west. What it was he could not rightly make out; he thought, perhaps, his senses deceived him; for, at other times, the sound had always come from the east where the sea was. But next morning, when it was Ravna's watch, Nansen was awakened by seeing the Finn's grimy face peering at him through an opening in the tent.

"Now, Ravna, what is it? can you see land?" he asked at a venture.

"Yes—yes—land too close!" croaked Ravna, as he drew his head back.

Nansen sprang out of the tent. Yes, there was the land, but a short distance off; and the ice was loose so that a way could easily be forced through it. In a twinkling all hands were busy; and a few hours later Nansen planted his foot on the firm land of Greenland.

1. Nordenskjöld (pron. Nordenshuld), famous Swedish explorer, discoverer of the North-east Passage.

2. Wille, another Norwegian, who at that time was professor at the High School in Stockholm.

3. Blaamand (pron. Blohmann).

4. One krone (crown) equals twenty-seven cents.

5. Storthing, the legislative assembly (congress) of Norway.

6. Folgefond, Jostedalsbræ, Svartisen, glaciers in Norway.

7. Karasjok (pron. Karashok), one of the northernmost districts of Norway, chiefly inhabited by Lapps.

8. Qvæn, the Norwegian name for a man of the race inhabiting the grand duchy of Finland. The Lapps are in Norway called Finns.

# Chapter V

Journey across Greenland.—Meeting Esquimaux.—Reaching the West Coast.—Return to Civilization and Home.

When Nansen and his companions, after their perilous adventures in the drift-ice, landed with flags flying on their boats on the east waste of Greenland, the first thing they did was to give vent to their feelings in a ringing hurrah—a sound which those wild and barren crags had never re-echoed before. Their joy, indeed, on feeling firm ground beneath their feet once more baffles description. In a word, they conducted themselves like a pack of schoolboys, singing, laughing, and playing all manner of pranks. The Lapps, however, did not partake in the general merriment, but took themselves off up the mountain-side, where they remained several hours.

But when their first ebullition of joy had somewhat subsided, Nansen himself followed the example of the Lapps, and clambered up the slope in order to get a good view over the landscape, leaving the others to prepare the banquet they determined to indulge in that evening on the sea-beach. And here he remained some little while, entranced with the wondrous beauty of the scene. The sea and the ice stretched far away to the east, shining like a belt of silver beneath him, while on the west the mountain-tops were bathed in a flood of hazy sunshine, and the inland ice, the "Sahara of the North," extended in a level unbroken plain for miles and miles into the interior.

A snow bunting perched on a stone close by him, and chirped a welcome; a mosquito came humming through the air to greet the stranger, and settled on his hand. He would not disturb it; it was a welcome from home. It wanted his blood, and he let it take its fill. To the south the grand outline of Cape Tordenskjold rose up in the horizon, its name and form recalling his country to his mind; and there arose in his breast an earnest desire, a deep longing, to sacrifice anything and everything for his beloved "Old Norway."

On rejoining his comrades, the feast was ready. It consisted of oatmeal biscuits, Gruyère cheese, whortleberry jam, and chocolate; and there is little doubt that these six adventurers "ate as one eats in the springtime of youth." For it had been unanimously resolved that, for this one day at least, they would enjoy themselves to the full; on the morrow their daily fare would be, to eat little, sleep little, and work as hard as possible. To-day, then, should be the first and the last of such indulgence. Time was precious!

On the next day, therefore, they resumed their northward journey, along the east coast, fighting their way day and night, inch by inch, foot by foot, through the drift-ice; at times in peril, at others in safety; past Cape Adelaer, past Cape Garde, ever forward in one incessant, monotonous struggle. And now they approached the ill-omened Puisortok, of which Esquimaux and European seafarers had many an evil tale to tell. There, it was said, masses of ice would either shoot up suddenly from beneath the surface of the water, and crush any vessel that ventured near, or would fall down from the overhanging height, and overwhelm it. There not a word must be spoken! there must be no laughing, no eating, no smoking, if one would pass it in safety! Above all, the fatal name of Puisortok must not pass the lips, else the glacier would be angry, and certain destruction ensue.

Nansen, however, it may be said, did not observe these regulations, and yet managed to pass it in safety. In his opinion there was nothing very remarkable or terrible about it.

But something else took place at Puisortok that surprised him and his companions.

On July 30, as they were preparing their midday meal, Nansen heard, amid the shrill cries of the seabirds, a strange weird sound. What it could be he could not conceive. It resembled the cry of a loon more than anything else, and kept coming nearer and nearer. Through his telescope, however, he discerned two dark specks among the ice-floes, now close together, now a little apart, making straight for them. They were human beings evidently—human beings in the midst of that desert region of ice, which they had thought to be a barren, uninhabited waste. Balto, too, watched their approach attentively, with a half astonished, half uneasy look, for he believed them to be supernatural beings.

On came the strangers, one of them bending forward in his kayak[1] as if bowing in salutation; and, on coming alongside the rock, they crawled out of their kayaks and stood before Nansen and his companions with bare heads, dressed in jackets and trousers of seal-skin, smiling, and making all manner of friendly gestures. They were Esquimaux, and had glass beads in their jet-black hair. Their skin was of a chestnut hue, and their movements, if not altogether graceful, were attractive.

On coming up to our travellers they began to ask questions in a strange language, which, needless to say, was perfectly unintelligible. Nansen, indeed, tried to talk to them in Esquimau from a conversation book in that tongue he had with him, but it was perfectly useless. And it was not till both parties had recourse to the language of signs that Nansen was able to ascertain that they belonged to an Esquimau encampment to the north of Puisortok.

These two Esquimaux were good-natured looking little beings; and now they began to examine the equipments of the travellers, and taste their food, with which they seemed beyond measure pleased, expressing their admiration at all they saw by a long-drawn kind of bovine bellow. Finally they took leave, and set off northward in their kayaks which they managed with wonderful dexterity, and soon disappeared from sight.

At six the same evening our travellers followed in the same direction, and in a short time reached the Esquimau encampment at Cape Bille. Long, however, before their eyes could detect any signs of tents or of human beings, their sense of smell became aware of a rank odor of train-oil, accompanied by a sound of voices; and they presently saw numbers of Esquimaux standing on the sea-beach, and on the rocks, earnestly watching the approach of the strangers.

It was a picturesque sight that presented itself to the eyes of our travellers.

"All about the ledges of the rocks," writes Nansen, "stood long rows of strangely wild, shaggy looking creatures, men, women and children—all dressed in much the same scanty attire, staring and pointing at us, and uttering the same cowlike sound we had heard in the forenoon. It was just as if a whole herd of cows were lowing one against another, as when the cowhouse door is opened in the morning to admit the expected fodder."

They were all smiling,—a smile indeed, is the only welcoming salute of the Esquimaux,—all eager to help Nansen and his companions ashore, chattering away incessantly in their own togue, like a saucepan boiling and bubbling over with words, not one of which, alas, could Nansen or his companions understand.

Presently Nansen was invited to enter one of their tents, in which was an odor of such a remarkable nature, such a blending of several ingredients, that a description thereof is impossible. It was the smell, as it were, of a mixture of train-oil, human exhalations, and the effluvium of fetid liquids all intimately mixed up together; while men and women, lying on the floor round the fire, children rolling about everywhere, dogs sniffing all around, helped to make up a scene that was decidedly unique.

*East Greenland Esquimaux*

All of the occupants were of a brownish-greyish hue, due mostly to the non-application of soap and water, and were swarming with vermin. All of them were shiny with train-oil, plump, laughing, chattering creatures—in a word, presenting a picture of primitive social life, in all its original blessedness.

Nansen does not consider the Esquimaux, crosseyed and flat-featured though they be, as by any means repulsive looking. The nose he describes, in the case of children, "as a depression in the middle of the face," the reverse ideal, indeed, of a European nose.

On the whole he considers their plump, rounded forms to have a genial appearance about them, and that the seal is the Esquimau prototype.

The hospitality of these children of nature was boundless. They would give away all they possessed, even to the shirt on their backs, had they possessed such an article; and certainly showed extreme gratitude when their liberality was reciprocated, evidently placing a high value on empty biscuit-tins, for each time any of them got one presented to him he would at once bellow forth his joy at the gift.

But what especially seemed to attract their interest was when Nansen and his companions began to undress, before turning in for the night into their sleeping-bags; while to watch them creep out of the same the next morning afforded them no less interest. They entertained, however, a great dread of the camera, for every time Nansen turned its dark glass eye upon them, a regular stampede would take place.

Next day Nansen and the Esquimaux parted company, some of the latter proceeding on their way to the south, others accompanying him on his journey northward. The leavetaking between the Esquimaux was peculiar, being celebrated by cramming their nostrils full of snuff from each other's snuff-horns. Snuff indeed is the only benefit, or the reverse, it seems the Esquimaux have derived from European civilization up to date; and is such a favorite, one might say necessary, article with them that they will go on a shopping expedition to the south to procure it, a journey that often takes them four years to accomplish!

---

The journey northward was an extremely fatiguing one, for they encountered such stormy weather that their boats more than once narrowly escaped being nipped in the ice. As a set-off, however, to this, the scenery proved to be magnificent,—the floating mountains of ice resembling enchanted castles, and all nature was on a stupendous scale. Finally they reached a harbor on Griffenfeldt's Island, where they enjoyed the first hot meal they had had on their coasting expedition, consisting of caraway soup. This meal of soup was a great comfort to the weary and worn-out travellers. Here a striking but silent testimony of that severe and pitiless climate presented itself in the form of a number of skulls and human bones lying blanched and scattered among the rocks, evidently the remains of Esquimaux who in times long gone by had perished from starvation.

After an incredible amount of toil, Nansen arrived at a small island in the entrance of the Inugsuazmuit Fjord, and thence proceeded to Skjoldungen where the water was more open. Here they encamped, and were almost eaten up by mosquitoes.

On Aug. 6 they again set out on their way northward, meeting with another encampment of Esquimaux, who were, however, so terrified at the approach of the strangers, that they one and all bolted off to the mountain, and it was not till Nansen presented them with an empty tin box and some needles that they became reassured, after which they accompanied the expedition for some little distance, and on parting gave Nansen a quantity of dried seal's flesh.

The farther our travellers proceeded on their journey, the more dissatisfied and uneasy did Balto and Ravna become. Accordingly one day Nansen took the opportunity of giving Balto a good scolding, who with tears and sobs gave vent to his complaints, "They had not had food enough—coffee only three times during the whole journey; and they had to work harder than any beast the whole livelong day, and he would gladly give many thousands of kroner to be safe at home once more."

There was indeed something in what Balto said. The fare had unquestionably been somewhat scanty, and the work severe; and it was evident that these children of nature, hardy though they were, could not vie with civilized people when it became a question of endurance for any length of time, and of risking life and taxing one's ability to the utmost.

Finally, on Aug. 10, the expedition reached Umivik in a dense fog, after a very difficult journey through the ice, and encamped for the last time on the east coast of Greenland. Here they boiled coffee, shot a kind of snipe, and lived like gentlemen, so that even Balto and Ravna were quite satisfied. The former, indeed, began intoning some prayers, as he had heard the priest in Finmarken do, in a very masterly manner,—a pastime, by the way, he never indulged in except he felt his life to be quite safe.

The next day, Aug. 11, rose gloriously bright. Far away among the distant glaciers a rumbling sound as of cannon could be heard, while snow-covered mountains towered high, overhead, on the other side of which lay boundless tracts of inland ice. Nansen and Sverdrup now made a reconnoitring expedition, and did not return till five o'clock the next morning. It still required some days to overhaul and get everything in complete order for their journey inland; and it was not till nine o'clock in the evening of Aug. 16, after first dragging up on land the boats, in which a few necessary articles of food were stored, together with a brief account of the progress of the expedition carefully packed in a tin box, that they commenced their journey across the inland ice.

Nansen and Sverdrup led the way with the large sleigh, while the others, each dragging a smaller one, followed in their wake. Thus these six men, confident of solving the problem before them, with the firm earth beneath their feet, commenced the ascent of the mountain-slope which Nansen christened "Nordenskjöld's Nunatak."[2]

Their work had now begun in real earnest—a work so severe and arduous that it would require all the strength and powers of endurance they possessed to accomplish it. The ice was full of fissures, and these had either to be circumvented or crossed, a very difficult matter with heavily laden sleighs. A covering of ice often lay over these fissures, so that great caution was required. Hence their progress was often very slow, each man being roped to his fellow; so that if one of them should happen to disappear into one of these fathomless abysses, his companion could haul him up. Such an occurrence happened more than once; for Nansen as well as the others would every now and then fall plump in up to the arms, dangling with his legs over empty space. But it always turned out well; for powerful hands took hold of the rope, and the practised gymnasts knew how to extricate themselves.

At first the ascent was very hard work, and it will readily be understood that the six tired men were not sorry on the first night of their journey to crawl into their sleeping-bags, after first refreshing the inner man with cup after cup of hot tea.

Yet, notwithstanding all the fatigue they had undergone, there was so much strength left in them that Dietrichson volunteered to go back and fetch a piece of Gruyère cheese they had left behind when halting for their midday meal. "It would be a nice little morning walk," he said, "before turning in!" And he actually went—all for the sake of a precious bit of cheese!

Next day there was a pouring rain that wet them through. The work of hauling the sleighs, however, kept them warm. But later in the evening, it came down in such torrents that Nansen deemed it advisable to pitch the tent, and here they remained, weather-bound, for three whole days. And long days they were! But our travellers followed the example of bruin in winter; that is, they lay under shelter the greater part of the time, Nansen taking care that they should also imitate bruin in another respect,—who sleeps sucking his paw,—by giving them rations once a day only. "He who does no work shall have little food," was his motto.

On the forenoon of the twentieth, however, the weather improved; and our travellers again set out on their journey, having first indulged in a good warm meal by way of recompense for their three days' fasting. The ice at first was very difficult, so much so that they had to retrace their steps, and, sitting on their sleighs, slide down the mountain slope. But the going improved, as also did the weather. "If it would only freeze a little," sighed Nansen. But he was to get enough of frost before long.

On they tramped, under a broiling sun, over the slushy snow. As there was no drinking-water to be had, they filled their flasks with snow, carrying them in their breast-pockets for the heat of their bodies to melt it.

On Aug. 22 there was a night frost; the snow was hard and in good condition, but the surface so rough and full of lumps and frozen waves of slush, that the ropes with which they dragged the sleighs cut and chafed their shoulders. "It was just as if our shoulders were being burnt," Balto said.

They now travelled mostly by night, for it was better going then, and there was no sun to broil them; while the aurora borealis, bathing as it were the whole of the frozen plain in a flood of silvery light, inspired them with fresh courage. The surface of the ice over which they travelled was as smooth and even as a lake newly frozen over. Even Balto on such occasions would indulge in a few oaths, a thing he never allowed himself except when he felt "master of the situation." He was a Finn, you see, and perhaps had no other way of giving expression to his feelings!

As they got into higher altitudes the cold at night became more intense. Occasionally they were overtaken by a snowstorm, when they had to encamp in order to avoid being frozen to death; while at times, again, the going would become so heavy in the fine drifting snow that they had to drag their sleighs one by one, three or four men at a time to each sleigh, an operation involving such tremendous exertion that Kristiansen, a man of few words, on one such occasion said to Nansen, "What fools people must be to let themselves in for work like this!"

To give some idea of the intense cold they had to encounter it may be stated that, at the highest altitude they reached,—9,272 feet above the sea,—the temperature fell to below -49° Fahrenheit, and this, too, in the tent at night, the thermometer being under Nansen's pillow. And all this toil and labor, be it remembered, went on from Aug. 16 to the end of September, with sleighs weighing on an average about two hundred and twenty pounds each, in drifting snow-dust, worse than even the sandstorms of Sahara.

In order to lighten their labor, Nansen resolved to use sails on the sleighs—a proceeding which Balto highly disapproved of: "Such mad people he had never seen before, to want to sail over the snow! He was a Lapp, he was, and there was nothing they could teach him on land. It was the greatest nonsense he had ever heard of!"

*Sledging across Greenland*

Sails, however, were forthcoming, notwithstanding Balto's objections; and they sat and stitched them with frozen fingers in the midst of the snow. But it was astonishing what a help they proved to be; and so they proceeded on their way, after slightly altering their course in the direction of Godthaab.[3]

Thus, then, we see these solitary beings, looking like dark spots moving on an infinite expanse of snow, wending their way ever onward, Nansen and Sverdrup side by side, ski-staff and ice-axe in hand, in front, earnestly gazing ahead as they dragged the heavy sleigh, while close behind followed Dietrichson and Kristiansen, Balto and Ravna bringing up the rear, each dragging a smaller sleigh. So it went on for weeks; and though it tried their strength, and put their powers of endurance to a most severe test, yet, if ever the thought of "giving it up" arose in their minds, it was at once scouted by all the party, the two Lapps excepted. One day Balto complained loudly to Nansen. "When you asked us," he said, "in

Christiania, what weight we could drag, we told you we could manage one hundredweight each, but now we have double that weight, and all I can say is, that, if we can drag these loads over to the west coast, we are stronger than horses."

Onward, however, they went, in spite of the cold, which at times was so intense that their beards froze fast to their jerseys, facing blinding snowstorms that well-nigh made old Ravna desperate. The only bright moments they enjoyed were when sleeping or at their meals. The sleeping-bags, indeed, were a paradise; their meals, ideals of perfect bliss.

Unfortunately, Nansen had not taken a sufficient supply of fatty food with him, and to such an extent did the craving for fat go, that Sverdrup one day seriously suggested that they should eat boot-grease—a compound of boiled grease and old linseed oil! Their great luxury was to eat raw butter, and smoke a pipe after it. First they would smoke the fragrant weed pure and simple; when that was done, the tobacco ash, followed by the oil as long as it would burn; and when this was all exhausted, they would smoke tarred yarn, or anything else that was a bit tasty! Nansen, who neither smoked nor chewed, would content himself with a chip of wood, or a sliver off one of the "truger" (snowshoes). "It tasted good," he said, "and kept his mouth moist."

Finally, on Sept. 14, they had reached their highest altitude, and now began to descend toward the coast, keeping a sharp lookout for "land ahead." But none was yet to be seen, and one day Ravna's patience completely gave way. With sobs and moans he said to Nansen,—

"I'm an old Fjeld-Lapp, and a silly old fool! I'm sure we shall never get to the coast!"

"Yes," was the curt answer, "it's quite true! Ravna is a silly old fool!"

One day, however, shortly afterward, while they were at dinner, they heard the twittering of a bird close by. It was a snow-bunting, bringing them a greeting from the west coast, and their hearts grew warm within them at the welcome sound.

On the next day, with sails set, they proceeded onward down the sloping ground, but with only partial success. Nansen was standing behind the large sleigh to steady it, while Sverdrup steered from the front. Merrily flew the bark; but, unfortunately, Nansen stumbled and fell, and had hard work to regain his legs, and harder work still to gather up sundry articles that had fallen off the sleigh, such as boxes of pemmican, fur jackets, and ice-axes. Meanwhile Sverdrup and the ship had almost disappeared from view, and all that Nansen could see of it was a dark, square speck, far ahead across the ice. Sverdrup had been sitting all the while in front, thinking what an admirable passage they were making, and was not a little astonished, on looking behind, to find that he was the only passenger on board. Matters, however, went on better after this; and in the afternoon, as they were sailing their best and fastest, the joyful cry of "Land ahead!" rang through the air. The west coast was in sight! After several days' hard work across fissures and over uneven ice, the coast itself was finally reached. But Godthaab was a long, long way off still, and to reach it by land was sheer impossibility.

The joy of our travellers on once more feeling firm ground beneath their feet, and of getting real water to drink, was indescribable. They swallowed quart after quart, till they could drink no more. The Lapps, as usual took themselves off to the fjeld to testify their joy.

That evening was the most delightful one they had experienced for weeks, one never to be forgotten in after years, when, with their tent pitched, and a blazing fire of wood, they sat beside it, Sverdrup smoking a pipe of moss in lieu of tobacco, and Nansen lying on his back on the grass, which shed a strange and delightful perfume all around.

But how was Godthaab to be reached? By land it was impossible! Therefore the journey must be made by sea! But there was no boat! A boat, then, must be built. And Sverdrup and Nansen were the men to solve the problem. They set to work, and by evening the boat was finished. Its dimensions were eight feet five inches in length, four feet eight inches in breadth, and it was made of willows and sail-cloth. The oars were of bamboo and willow branches, across the blades of which canvas was stretched. The thwarts were made from bamboo, and the foot of one of their scientific instruments which, by the way, chafed them terribly, and were very uncomfortable seats.

*On the way to Godthaab*

All preparations being now made, Nansen and Sverdrup set off on their adventurous journey. The first day it was terribly hard work, for the water was too shallow to admit of rowing. On the second day, however, they put out to sea. Here they had at times to encounter severe weather, fearing every moment lest their frail bark should be swamped or capsized. At night they would sleep on the naked shore beneath the open sky. From morning till night struggling away with their oars, living on hot soup and the sea-birds they shot, which were ravenously devoured without much labor being devoted to cooking the same. Finally they reached their destination, meeting with a hearty welcome, accompanied by a salute from cannon fired off in their honor, when once it was ascertained who the new arrivals were.

Nansen's first inquiry was about a ship for Denmark, and he learned, to his great disappointment, that the last vessel for the season had sailed from Godthaab two months before, and that the nearest ship, the Fox, was lying at Ivitgut, three hundred miles off.

It was a terrible blow in the midst of their joy. Home had, as it were, at one stroke receded many hundreds of miles away; and here they would have to pass a whole winter and spring, while dear ones at home would think they had perished, and would be mourning for their supposed loss all those weary months.

But this must never be! The Fox must be got at, and friends at home must at all events get letters by her.

After a great deal of trouble Nansen at length found an Esquimau who agreed to set off in his kayak bearing two letters. One was from Nansen to Gamel, who had equipped the expedition; the other from Sverdrup to his father.

This having been arranged, and boats having been sent off to fetch their comrades from Ameralikfjord, Nansen and Sverdrup plunged into all the joys and delights of civilized life to which they had so long been strangers. Now they were able to indulge in the luxury of soap and water for the first time since the commencement of their journey across the ice. To change their clothes, to sleep in proper beds, to eat civilized food with knives and forks on earthenware plates, to smoke, to converse with educated beings, was to them the summum bonum of enjoyment, and they felt themselves to be in clover.

Notwithstanding all these, Nansen did not seem altogether himself. He was in a dreamy state, thinking perhaps of nights spent in sleeping-bags up on the inland ice, or dreaming of that memorable evening in the Ameralikfjord, of the hard struggles they had undergone on the boundless plains of snow. These things flashed across him, excluding from his mind the conviction that he had rendered his name famous.

At last, on Oct. 12, the other members of the expedition joined them, and these six men, who had risked their lives in that perilous adventure, were once more assembled together.

His object had been attained, and the name of Fridtjof Nansen would soon be known the whole world over!

That same autumn the Fox brought to Norway tidings of the success of the expedition, and a few hours after her arrival the telegraph announced throughout the length and breadth of the civilized world, in few but significant words, "Fridtjof Nansen has crossed over the inland ice of Greenland."

And the Norwegian nation, which had refused to grant the venturesome young man 5,000 kroner ($1,350), now raised her head, and called Fridtjof Nansen one of her best sons. And when one day in April, after having spent a long winter in Greenland, he went on board the Hvidbjörn[4] on his homeward journey, preparations were being made in the capital for a festival such as a king receives when he visits his subjects.

It was May 30: the spring sun was shining with all its brilliancy over Norway. The Christiania fjord was teeming with yachts and small sailing-boats. A light breeze played over the ruffled surface of the water, while the perfume of the budding trees on its banks shed a sweet fragrance all around. As for the town, it literally swarmed with human beings. The quays, the fortress, the very roofs of the houses, were densely packed with eager crowds, all of them intently gazing seaward. Presently a shout of welcome heard faintly in the distance announced his approach, gradually increasing in volume as he came nearer, till it merged into one continuous roar, while thousands of flags were waving overhead.

Eagerly the crowds pressed forward to catch the first glimpse of his form, and when they did recognize him, their hurrahs burst forth like a storm, and were caught up in the streets, answered from the windows, from the tops of houses; and when they ceased for a moment from the sheer exhaustion of those who uttered them, they were soon renewed with redoubled vigor. And when finally Nansen had disembarked and had entered a carriage, the police could no longer keep the people under control. As if with one accord they dashed forward, and taking out the horses, harnessed themselves in their place, and dragged him through the streets of the city in triumph.

Yes, the Norwegian people had taken possession of Fridtjof Nansen!

But up at a window there stood the old housekeeper from Store Fröen, waving her white apron, while tears of joy trickled down her face. She it was who had bound up his bleeding head when years ago he had fallen and cut it on the ice; she it was to whom he had often gone when in some childish scrape. He remembered her in his hour of triumph. And as she was laughing and crying by turns, and waving her apron, he dashed up the steps and gave her a loving embrace.

For was she not part and parcel of his home?

---

1. Kayak, small and light boat, chiefly made of sealskin, used by the natives of Greenland.
2. Peaks of rock projecting above the surface of the ice.
3. Godthaab (pron. Gott-hōb), the only city, and seat of the Danish governor, on the west coast of Greenland.
4. Hvidbjörn (pron. Vid-byurn), The White Bear, a trading-vessel.

# Chapter VI

Engagement and Marriage.—Home-Life.—Planning the Polar Expedition.

Two months after Nansen had returned home from his Greenland expedition he became engaged to Eva Sars, daughter of the late Professor Sars, and was married to her the same autumn. Her mother was the sister of the poet Welhaven.

The following story of his engagement is related:—

"On the night of Aug. 12 a shower of gravel and small pebbles rattled against the panes of a window in the house where Fridtjof Nansen's half-sister lived. He was very fond of her, and of her husband also, who had indeed initiated him in the use of gun and rod, and who had taken him with him, when a mere lad, on many a sporting excursion to Nordmarken.

"On hearing this unusual noise at the dead of night, his brother-in-law jumped out of bed in no very amiable frame of mind, and opening the window, called out, 'What is it?'

"'I want to come in!' said a tall figure dressed in gray, from the street below.

"A volley of expletives greeted the nocturnal visitor, who kept on saying, 'I want to come in.'

"Before long Fridtjof Nansen was standing in his sister's bedroom at two o'clock in the morning.

"Raising herself up in the bed, she said, 'But, Fridtjof, whatever is it?'
"'I'm engaged to be married—that's all!' was the laconic reply.
"'Engaged! But with whom?'
"'Why, with Eva, of course!'

"Then he said he felt very hungry, and his brother-in-law had to take a journey into the larder and fetch out some cold meat, and then down into the cellar after a bottle of champagne. His sister's bed served for a table, and a new chapter in 'Fridtjof's saga' was inaugurated at this nocturnal banquet."

The story goes, Nansen first met his future wife in a snowdrift. One day, it appears, when up in the Frogner woods, he espied two little boots sticking up out of the snow. Curiosity prompted him to go and see to whom the said boots belonged, and as he approached for that purpose, a little snow be-sprinkled head peered up at him. It was Eva Sars!

What gives this anecdote interest is that it was out of the snow and the cold to which he was to dedicate his life, she, who became dearer to him than life itself, first appeared.

Another circumstance connected therewith worthy of note is that Eva Sars was a person of rather a cold and repellent nature, and gave one the impression that there was a good deal of snow in her disposition. Hence the reason perhaps why she kept aloof rather than attracted those who would know her. Fridtjof Nansen, however, was not the man to be deterred by coldness. He was determined to win her, even if he should have to cross the inland ice of Greenland for that purpose.

But when she became his wife all the reserve and coldness of her nature disappeared. She took the warmest interest in his plans, participated in his work, making every sacrifice a woman can make to promote his purpose. In all his excursions in the open air she accompanied him; and when she knew that he was making preparations for another expedition, one involving life itself, not a murmur escaped her lips. And when the hour of parting came at last, and a long, lonely time of waiting lay before her, she broke out into song. For in those dreary years of hope deferred she developed into an accomplished songstress; and when the fame of Nansen's exploit resounded throughout the whole north, the echo of her song answered in joyful acclaim. The maidens of Norway listening to her spirited strains, and beholding this brave little woman with her proudly uplifted head, learnt from Eva Nansen that such was the way in which a woman should meet a sorrow—such the way in which she should undergo a time of trial.

The following story, in Nansen's own words, will serve to give an idea of the sort of woman she was:

"It was New Year's Eve, 1890. Eva and I had gone on a little trip to Kröderen,[1] and we determined to get to the top of Norefjeld. "We slept at Olberg, and, feeling rather lazy next morning, did not set out till nearly noon. We took it very easily, moreover! Even in summer-time it is a stiff day's work to clamber up Norefjeld; but in winter, when the days are short, one has to look pretty sharp to reach the top while it is light. Moreover, the route we chose, though perhaps the most direct, was not by any means the shortest. The snow lay very deep; and soon it became impossible to go on ski, the ascent being so steep, that we had to take them off and carry them. However, we had made up our minds to reach the top; for it would never do to turn back after having gone half-way, difficult though the ascent might be. The last part of our journey was the most trying of all; I had to cut out steps with my ski-staff to get a foothold in the frozen snow. I went in front, and Eva followed close behind me. It really seemed that we slipped two steps backward for every one we took forward. At last we reached the top; it was pitch dark, and we had been going from ten A.M. to five P.M., without food. But, thank goodness, we had some cheese and pemmican with us, so we sat down on the snow, and ate it.

"Yes! there were we two alone on the top of Norefjeld, five thousand feet above the sea, with a biting wind blowing that made our cheeks tingle, and the darkness growing thicker and thicker every moment. Far away in the west there was a faint glimmer of daylight,—of the last day of the old year,—just enough to guide us by. The next thing to be done was to get down to Eggedal. From where we were it was a distance of about six and one-half miles, a matter of little consequence in broad daylight, but in the present instance no joke, I can assure you! However, it had to be done. So off we started, I leading the way, Eva following.

"We went like the wind down the slope, but had to be very careful. When one has been out in the dark some little time, it is just as if the snow gives out a faint light—though light it cannot really be termed, but a feeble kind of shimmer. Goodness only knows how we managed to get down, but get down we did! As it was too steep to go on ski, there was nothing for it but to squat and slide down—a kind of locomotion detrimental, perhaps, to one's breeches, but under the circumstances unquestionably the safest mode of proceeding in the dark!

"When we had got half-way down my hat blew off. So I had to 'put the brake on,' and get up on my legs, and go after it. Far away above me I got a glimpse of a dark object on the snow, crawled after it, got up to it, and grasped it, to find it was only a stone! My hat, then, must be further up. Surely that was it—again I got hold of a stone! The snow seemed to be alive with stones. Hat after hat, hat after hat, but whenever I tried to put it on my head, it turned out to be a stone. A stone for bread is bad enough, and stones for hats are not a bit better! So I had to give it up, and go hatless.

"Eva had been sitting waiting for me all this while. 'Eva,' I shouted, and a faint answer came back from below.

"Those miles seemed to be uncommonly long ones. Every now and then we could use our ski, and then it would become so steep again that we had to carry them. At last we came to a standstill. There was a chasm right in front of us,—how deep it was it was too dark to ascertain. However, we bundled over it somehow or other, and happily the snow was very deep. It is quite incredible how one can manage to get over a difficulty!

"As regards our direction, we had lost it completely; all we knew was that we must get down into the valley. Again we came to a standstill, and Eva had to wait while I went on, groping in the dark, trying to find a way. I was absent on this errand some little time. Presently it occurred to me, 'What if she should have fallen asleep!'

"'Eva!' I shouted, 'Eva!' Yes, she answered; but she must be a long way above where I was. If she had been asleep it would have been a difficult matter to have found her. But I groped my way up-hill to her, with the consolation that I had found the bed of a stream. Now the bed of a stream is not very well adapted for ski, especially when it is pitch dark, and the stomach is empty, and conscience pricks you,—for really I ought not to have ventured on such an expedition with her. However, 'all's well that ends well,' and we got through all right.

"We had now got down to the birch scrub, and at last found our road.

"After some little time we passed a cabin. I thought it wouldn't be a bad place to take refuge in, but Eva said it was so horribly dirty! She was full of spirits now, and voted for going on. So on we went, and in due time reached the parish clerk's house in Eggedal. Of course the inmates were in bed, so we had to arouse them. The clerk was horrified when I told him we had just come from the top of Norefjeld. This time Eva was not so nice about lodgings, for no sooner had she sat down on a chair, than she fell asleep. It was midnight, mind you, and she had been in harness fourteen hours.

"'He's a bit tired, poor lad!' said the clerk. For Eva had on a ski-dress with a very small skirt, trousers, and a Lapp fur cloak.

"'That's my wife,' I replied, whereupon he burst out into a laugh. 'Nay, nay! to drag his wife with him over the top of Norefjeld on New Year's Eve!' he said.

"Presently he brought in something to eat, for we were famished; and when Eva smelt it wasn't cheese and pemmican, she woke up.

"We rested here three days. Yes, it had been a New Year's Eve trip. A very agreeable one in my opinion, but I'm not so sure Eva altogether agreed with me!

"Two days later I and the 'poor little lad' drove through Numedal to Kongsberg in nine degrees below zero (Fahrenheit), which nearly froze the little fellow. But it is not a bad thing occasionally to have to put up with some inconveniences—you appreciate comforts afterward so much the more. He who has never experienced what cold is, does not really know the meaning of warmth!"

---

The day after the wedding the newly married pair set out for Newcastle, where there was to be a meeting of the Geographical Society, travelling via Gothenburg, Hamburg, and London. After this they went to Stockholm, and here Nansen was presented with the "Vega" medal by His Majesty. This was a distinguished honor, the more so as it had hitherto only been awarded to five persons, among whom were Stanley and Nordenskjöld. Nansen subsequently was presented with several medals in foreign countries, and was made a Knight of the Order of St. Olaf and Danebrog.

On their return from Stockholm to Norway, Nansen and his wife took apartments at Marte Larsen's, the old housekeeper at Store Fröen, and stayed there two months, after which they took a house on the Drammen road. But they did not enjoy themselves there, and Nansen determined to build a house, for which purpose he bought a site at Svartebugta, near Lysaker.[2] It was here that, as a boy, he had often watched for wild ducks. It was a charming spot, moreover, and within easy distance of the town. The house was finished in the spring of 1890. During the whole of the winter, while building operations were going on, they lived in an icy cold pavillion near Lysaker railway station.

"It was here he weaned me from freezing," says Eva Nansen.

In this wretched habitation, where the water froze in the bedroom at night, Nansen would sit and work at his book on Greenland, and when he had time would superintend the building of the new house. It was called "Godthaab"—a name given it by Björnstjerne Björnson.

In the autumn of this year Nansen set out on a lengthened lecturing tour, accompanied by his wife. He lectured in Copenhagen, London,

Berlin, and Dresden, about his Greenland experiences, and also about the projected expedition to the North Pole. Everywhere people were attracted by his captivating individuality; but most thought this new expedition too venturesome. Even the most experienced Arctic explorers shook their heads, for they thought that, from such a daring enterprise, not a single member of the expedition would ever return alive.

But Nansen adhered to his own opinions, and we see him in the intervening years occupied with the equipment required for an expedition to the polar regions—a work so stupendous that the preparations for the Greenland expedition were but child's play in comparison.

---

1. Kröderen, a lake about forty miles to the northwest of Christiania. Norefjeld, a mountain on the west side of the lake. Olberg, a farmhouse at the foot of the mountain.
2. Lysaker, a railroad station about four miles west of Christiania.

# Chapter VII

Preparations for the Polar Expedition.—Starting from Norway.—
Journey along the Siberian Coast.

Nansen's theory as regards the expedition to the North Pole was as simple as it was daring. He believed that he had discovered the existence of a current passing over the pole, and of this he would avail himself. His idea, in fact, was to work his way into the ice among the New Siberian Islands, let his vessel be fast frozen into the drift-ice, and be carried by the current over the Pole to the east coast of Greenland. There articles had been found on ice-floes that had unquestionably belonged to former Arctic expeditions, a fact that convinced him of the existence of such a current.

It might take some years for a vessel to drift all that way; he must, therefore, make his preparations accordingly. Such at all events was Nansen's theory—a theory which, it must be said, few shared with him. For none of the world's noted explorers of those regions believed in the existence of such a current, and people generally termed the scheme, "a madman's idea!"

Nansen, therefore, stood almost alone in this, and yet not altogether alone, either. For the Norwegian people who would not sacrifice $1,350 for the Greenland expedition gave him now in a lump sum 280,000 kroner ($75,600). They were convinced of his gigantic powers, and when the Norwegians are fully convinced of a thing, they are willing to make any sacrifice to carry it out. They believed in him now!

Nansen then set to work in earnest at his gigantic undertaking.

First of all a vessel must be designed,—one that would be able to defy the ice. Availing himself, therefore, of the services of the famous shipbuilder, Colin Archer, he had the Fram[1] built—a name suggestive of noble achievements to the youth of Norway.

On Oct. 26, 1892, she was launched at Laurvig. During the previous night the temperature had been fourteen degrees above zero, and a slight sprinkling of snow had covered valley and height with a thin veil of white. The morning sun peered through the mist with that peculiar hazy light that foretells a bright winter day.

At the station at Laurvig, Nansen waited to receive his guests. A whaler, with a crow's-nest on her foretop, was lying in the harbor, to convey the visitors to the spot where the Fram was lying on the stocks.

In the bay at Reykjavik the huge hull of a vessel may be seen raised up on the beach, with her stern toward the sea. It is Fridtjof Nansen's new ship that is now to be launched. She is a high vessel, of great beam, painted black below and white above. Three stout masts of American pitch-pine are lying by her side on the quay, while three flagstaffs, two of them only with flags flying, rear themselves up aloft on her deck. The flag which is to be run up the bare staff is to bear the vessel's name—unknown as yet. Everybody is wondering what that name will be, and conjectures whether it will be Eva, Leif, Norway, Northpole, are rife.

Crowds of spectators are assembled at the wharf, while as many have clambered upon the adjacent rocks. But around the huge ship, which lies on the slips firmly secured with iron chains, are standing groups of stalwart, weather-beaten men in working attire. They are whalers, who for years have frequented the polar seas and braved its dangers, and are now attentively examining and criticising the new ship's construction. A goodly number, too, of workmen are there,—the men who built the ship; and they are looking at their work with feelings of pride. And yonder is the vessel's architect,—that stately, earnest-looking man with the long, flowing white beard,—Colin Archer.

And now, accompanied by his wife, Nansen ascends the platform that has been erected in the ship's bow. Mrs. Nansen steps forward, breaks a bottle of champagne on the prow, and in clear, ringing tones declares, "Fram is her name." At the same moment a flag on which the vessel's name can be read in white letters on a red ground, is run up to the top of the bare flagstaff.

The last bands and chains are quickly removed, and the ponderous mass glides, stern first, slowly down the incline, but with ever-increasing velocity, toward the water. For a moment some anxiety is felt lest she should sink or get wedged; but as soon as her bows touch the water the stern rises up, and the Fram floats proudly on the sea, and is then at once moored fast with warps to the quay.

*Crew of the Fram*
*By permission of Harper & Brothers*

Meanwhile Nansen stood beside his wife, and all eyes turned toward them. But not a trace of anxiety or doubt could be discerned on his frank and open countenance; for he possessed that faith in his project that is able to remove mountains.

The next matter of importance was to select the crew. There was ample material to choose from, for hundreds of volunteers from abroad offered themselves, besides Norwegians. But it was a Norwegian expedition—her crew, then, must be exclusively a national crew! And so Otto Sverdrup, who had earned his laurels in the Greenland expedition; Sigurd Scott-Hansen, first lieutenant in the royal navy; Henrik Greve Blessing, surgeon; Theodor Claudius Jacobsen and Adolf Juell of the mercantile marine; Anton Amundsen and Lars Petterson, engineers; Frederik Hjalmar Johansen, lieutenant of the royal army reserve, Peter Leonard Henriksen, harpooner; Bernt Nordahl, electrician; Ivar Otto Irgens Mogstad, head keeper at the lunatic asylum; and Bernt Berntsen, common sailor,—were selected. Most of them were married and had children.

Sverdrup was to be the Fram's commander, for Nansen knew that the ship would be safer in his hands than in his own.

Finally, after an incredible deal of hard work in getting everything in order, the day of their departure arrived.

It was midsummer—a dull, gloomy day. The Fram, heavily laden, is lying at Pipperviken Quay, waiting for Nansen. The appointed hour is past, and yet there are no signs of him. Members of the storthing, who had assembled there to bid him farewell, can wait no longer, and the crowds of people that line the quay are one and all anxiously gazing over the fjord.

But presently a quick-sailing little petroleum boat heaves in sight. It swings round Dyna,[2] and quickly lies alongside the Fram; and Nansen goes on board his ship at once, and gives the order to "go ahead." Every eye is fixed on him. He is as calm as ever, firm as a rock, but his face is pale.

The anchor is weighed; and after making the tour of the little creek, the Fram steams down the fjord. "Full speed" is the command issued from the bridge; and as she proceeds on her way, Nansen turns round to take a farewell look over Svartebugta where Godthaab lies. He discerns a glimpse of a woman's form dressed in white by the bench under the fir-tree, and then turns his face away; it was there he had bidden her farewell. Little Liv, his only child, had been carried by her mother, crowing and smiling, to bid father good-by, and he had taken her in his arms.

"Yes, you smile, little one!" he said; "but I"—and he sobbed.

This had taken place but an hour before. And now he was standing on the bridge alone, leaving all he held dear behind.

The twelve men who accompanied him,—they, too, had made sacrifices,—each had his own sorrow to meet at this hour; but at the word of command, one and all went about their duty as if nothing was amiss.

For the first few days it was fine weather, but on getting out as far as Lindesnæs[3] it became very stormy. The ship rolled like a log, and seas broke over the rails on both sides. Great fear was entertained lest the deck cargo should be carried overboard, a contingency, indeed, that soon occurred; for twenty-five empty paraffin casks broke loose from their lashings, and a quantity of reserve timber balks followed.

"It was an anxious time," says Nansen. "Seasick I stood on the bridge, alternately offering libations to the gods of the sea, and trembling for the safety of the boats and of the men who were trying to make snug what they could on deck. Now a green sea poured over us, and knocked one fellow off his legs so that he was deluged; now the lads were jumping over hurtling spars to avoid getting their feet crushed. There was not a dry thread on them. Juell was lying asleep in the 'Grand Hotel,' as we called one of the long boats, and awoke to find the sea roaring under him. I met him at the cabin door as he came running down. Once the Fram buried her bows and shipped a sea over the forecastle. One fellow was clinging to the anchor davits over the foaming water; it was poor Juell again."

Then all the casks, besides a quantity of timber, had to be thrown overboard. It was, indeed, an anxious time.

But fine weather came at last, and Bergen turned out to meet them in brilliant sunshine. Then on again, along the wonderful coast of Norway, while the people on shore stood gazing after them, marvelling as they passed.

At Beian[4] Sverdrup joined the ship, and Berntsen, the thirteenth member of the crew, at Tromsö.[5]

Still onward toward the north, till finally the last glimpse of their native country faded from their sight in the hazy horizon, and a dense fog coming on enveloped them in its shroud. They were to have met the Urania, laden with coal, in Jugor straits; but as that vessel had not arrived, and time was precious, the Fram proceeded on her course, after having shipped a number of Esquimau dogs which a Russian, named Trontheim, had been commissioned to procure for the expedition. It was here that Nansen took leave of his secretary, Cristophersen, who was to return by the Urania; and the last tie that united them with Norway was severed.

The Fram now heads out from the Jugor straits into the dreaded Kara sea, which many had prophesied would be her destruction. But they worked their way through storm and ice, at times satisfactorily, at others encountering slight mishaps; but the Fram proved herself to be a reliable iceworthy vessel, and Nansen felt more and more convinced that, when the ice-pressure began in real earnest, she would acquit herself well.

"It was a royal pleasure," he writes, "to take her into difficult ice. She twists and turns like a ball on a plate—and so strong! If she runs into a floe at full speed, she scarcely utters a sound, only quivers a little, perhaps."

When, as was often the case, they had to anchor on account of bad weather, Nansen and his companions would go ashore, either for the purpose of taking observations or for sport. One day they shot two bears and sundry reindeer; but, when they started to row back to the Fram in the evening, they had a severe task before them. For a strong breeze was blowing, and the current was dead against them. "We rowed as if our finger-tips would burst," says Nansen, "but could hardly make any headway. So we had to go in under land again to get out of the current. But no sooner did we set out for the Fram again than we got into it once more, and then the whole manœuvre had to be repeated, with the same result. Presently a buoy was lowered from the ship: if we could only reach it, all would be right. But no such luck was in store for us yet. We would make one more desperate effort, and we rowed with a will, every muscle of our bodies strained to the utmost. But to our vexation we now saw the buoy being hauled up. We rowed a little to the windward of the Fram, and then tried again to sheer over. This time we got nearer her than we had been before, but still no buoy was thrown over—not even a man was to be seen on deck. We roared like madmen," writes Nansen, "for a buoy—we had no strength left for another attempt. It was not a pleasing prospect to have to drift back, and go ashore again in our wet clothes,—we would get on board! Once more we yelled like wild Indians, and now they came rushing aft, and threw out the buoy in our direction. We put our last strength into our oars. There were only a few boat-lengths to cover, and the lads bent flat over the thwarts. Now only three boat-lengths. Another desperate spurt! Now only two and a half boat-lengths—presently two—then only one! A few more frantic pulls, and there was a little less. 'Now, my lads, one or two more hard pulls—keep to it!—Now another—don't give in—one more—there we have it!' And a joyful sigh of relief passed round the boat. 'Keep her going, or the rope will break—row, my lads!' And row we did, and soon they had hauled us alongside the Fram. Not till we were lying there, getting our bearskins and flesh hauled on board, did we realize what we had had to fight against. The current was running along the side of the ship like a millstream. At last we were on board. It was evening by this time, and it was a comfort to get some hot food, and then stretch one's limbs in a comfortable, dry berth."

The Fram proceeded on her course the next day, passing a number of unknown islands, to which Nansen gave names. Among these were Scott-Hansen's Islands, Ringnes, Mohns, etc.

On Sept. 6, the anniversary of Nansen's wedding, they passed Taimar Island, and after a prosperous passage through open water reached Cape Tscheljuskin on Sept. 9.

Nansen was sitting in the crow's nest that evening. The weather was perfectly still, and the sky lay in a dream of gold and yellow. A solitary star was visible; it stood directly over Cape Tscheljuskin, twinkling brightly, though sadly, in the pale sky overhead. As the vessel proceeded on her course it seemed to follow them. There was something about that star that attracted Nansen's attention, and brought him peace. It was as it were his star, and he felt that she who was at home was sending him a message by it. Meanwhile the Fram toiled on through the gloomy melancholy of the night out into the unknown.

In the morning, when the sun rose up, a salute was fired, and high festival held on board.

A few days later a herd of walrus was sighted. It was a lovely morning, and perfectly calm, so that they could distinctly hear their bellowings over the clear surface of the water, as they lay in a heap on an ice-floe, the blue mountains glittering in the sunlight in the background.

"My goodness, what a lot of meat!" ejaculated Juell, the cook. And at once Nansen, Juell, and Henriksen set out after them, Juell rowing, Nansen armed with a gun, and Henriksen with a harpoon. On getting to close quarters Henriksen threw the harpoon at the nearest walrus, but it struck too high, and glanced off the tough hide, and went skipping over the rounded backs of the others. Now all was stir and life. Ten or a dozen of the bulky animals waddled with upraised heads to the extreme edge of the floe, whereupon Nansen took aim at the largest, and fired. The brute staggered, and fell headlong into the water. Another bullet into a second walrus was attended with the same result, and the rest of the herd plunged into the water, so that it boiled and seethed. Soon, however, they were up again, all around the boat, standing upright in the water, bellowing and roaring till the air shook. Every now and then they would make a dash toward the boat, then dive, and come up again. The sea boiled like a cauldron, and every moment they seemed about to dash their tusks through the side of the boat, and capsize it. Fortunately, however, this did not occur. Walrus after walrus was shot by Nansen, while Henriksen was busy with his harpoon to prevent them sinking.

At last, after a favorable journey through open water, the Fram finally reached firm ice on Sept. 25, and allowed herself to be frozen in; for winter was fast approaching, and it was no longer possible to drive her through the ice.

1. Fram means onward.
2. Dyna, an islet with a lighthouse in Christiania harbor.
3. Cape Lindesnæs, the southernmost point of Norway.
4. Beian (pron. By-an), a village and stopping-place for the coast-wise steamers in northern Norway, near Trondhjem.
5. Tromsö, the chief city and bishop's see of the bishopric of same name, the northernmost diocese in Norway.

# Chapter VIII

Drifting Through the Ice.—Christmas.—Daily Life on the Fram.—
Bear-Hunt and Ice-Pressure.

From Sept. 26 the Fram lay frozen in in the drift-ice, and many a long day would pass ere she would be loose again. Nansen's theory of a current over the North Pole would now be proved to be correct or the reverse.

It was a monotonous time that was approaching for the men on board. At first they drifted but very little northward, each succeeding day bringing but little alteration; but they kept a good heart, for they had not to suffer from lack of anything that could conduce to their comfort. They had a good ship, excellently equipped, and so passed the days as best they could,—now occupying themselves with seeing to the dogs or taking observations, etc.; while reading, playing cards, chess, halma, and making all kinds of implements, filled up the remainder of their time. Every now and then the monotony of their existence would undergo variation, when the ice-pressure set in. Then there was plenty of life and stir on board, and all hands would turn out to do battle with the foe.

*The Fram in an Ice Pressure*
*By permission of Harper & Brothers*

It was on Monday, Oct. 9, that the Fram underwent her first experience of a regular ice-pressure. Nansen and the others were sitting after dinner, as usual, chatting about one thing and another, when all at once a deafening sound was heard, and the ship quivered from stem to stern. Up they rushed on deck; for now the Fram was to be put to the test—and gloriously she passed through it! When the ice nipped she lifted herself up, as if raised by invisible hands, and pushed the floes down below her.

An ice-pressure is a most wonderful thing. Let us hear what Nansen says of it:—

"It begins with a gentle crack and moan along the ship's sides, gradually sounding louder in every conceivable key. Now it is a high plaintive tone, now it is a grumble, now it is a snarl, and the ship gives a start up. Steadily the noise increases till it is like all the pipes of an organ; the ship trembles and shakes, and rises by fits and starts, or is gently lifted up. But presently the uproar slackens, and the ship sinks down into her old position again, as if in a safe bed."

But woe to them who have not such a ship to resort to under a pressure like this; for when once it begins in real earnest, it is as if there could not be a spot on the earth's surface that would not tremble and shake.

"First," says Nansen, "you hear a sound like the thundering rumble of an earthquake far away on the great waste; then you hear it in several places, always coming nearer and nearer. The silent ice world re-echoes with thunders; nature's giants are awakening to the battle. The ice cracks on every side of you, and begins to pile itself up in heaps. There are howlings and thunderings around you; you feel the ice trembling, and hear it rumbling under your feet. In the semi-darkness you can see it piling and tossing itself up into high ridges,—floes ten, twelve, fifteen feet thick, broken and flung up on the top of each other,—you jump away to save your life. But the ice splits in front of you; a black gulf opens, and the water streams up. You turn in another direction; but there through the dark you can just see a new ridge of moving ice-blocks coming toward you. You try another direction, but there it is just the same. All around there is thundering and roaring, as of some enormous waterfall with explosions like cannon salvoes. Still nearer you it comes. The floe you are standing on gets smaller and smaller; water pours over it; there can be no escape except by scrambling over the ice-blocks to get to the other side of the pack. But little by little the disturbance calms down again, and the noise passes on and is lost by degrees in the distance."

Another thing brought life and stir into the camp, viz., "bears." And many a time the cry of "bears" was heard in those icy plains.

In Farthest North, Nansen describes a number of amusing incidents with these animals. We must, however, content ourselves with giving only a brief sketch of some of the most interesting of these.

Nansen and Sverdrup, and indeed several of the others, had shot polar bears before; but some of their number were novices in the sport, among whom were Blessing, Johansen and Scott-Hansen. One day, when the latter were taking observations a short distance from the ship, a bear was seen but a little way off—in fact, just in front of the Fram.

"Hush! don't make a noise, or we shall frighten him," said Hansen; and they all crouched down to watch him.

"I think I'd better slip off on board and tell them about it," said Blessing. And off he started on tiptoe, so as not to alarm the bear.

The beast meanwhile came sniffing and shambling along toward where they were, so that evidently he had not been frightened.

Catching sight of Blessing, who was slinking off to the ship, the brute made straight for him.

Blessing, seeing that the bear was by no means alarmed, now made his way back to his companions as quickly as he could, closely followed by the bear. Matters began to look rather serious, and they each snatched up their weapons. Hansen, an ice-staff, Johansen, an axe, and Blessing nothing at all, shouting at the top of their voices, "Bear! bear!" after which they all took to their heels as fast as ever they could for the ship. The bear, however, held on his course toward the tent, which he examined very closely before following on their tracks. The animal was subsequently shot on approaching the Fram. Nansen was not a little surprised on finding in its stomach a piece of paper stamped, "Lutken & Mohn, Christiania," which he recognized as belonging to the ship.

On another occasion, toward the end of 1893, Hendriksen, whose business it was to see to the dogs that were tethered on an ice-floe, came tearing into the ship, and shouting, "Come with a gun! Come with a gun!" The bear, it seems, had bitten him on his side. Nansen immediately caught up his gun, as also did Hendriksen, and off they set after the bear. There was a confused sound of human voices on the starboard side of the ship, while on the ice below the gangway the dogs were making a tremendous uproar.

Nansen put his gun up to his shoulder, but it wouldn't go off. There was a plug of tow in the barrel. And Hendriksen kept crying out, "Shoot, shoot! mine won't go off!" There he stood clicking and clicking, for his gun was stuffed up with vaseline. Meanwhile the bear was lying close under the ship, worrying one of the dogs. The mate, too, was fumbling away at his gun, which was also plugged, while Mogstad, the fourth man, was brandishing an empty rifle, for he had shot all his cartridges away, crying out, "Shoot him! shoot him!" The fifth man, Scott-Hansen, was lying in the passage leading into the chart-room, groping after cartridges through a narrow chink in the door; for Kvik's kennel stood against it, so that he could not get it wide open. At last, however, Johansen came, and fired right into the bear's hide. This shot had the effect of making the brute let go of the dog, which jumped up and ran away. Several shots were now fired, which killed the bear.

Hendriksen tells this story about his being bitten:—

"You see," he said, "as I was going along with the lantern, I saw some drops of blood by the gangway, but thought one of the dogs had very likely cut its foot. On the ice, however, we saw bear-tracks, and started off to the west, the whole pack of dogs with us running on ahead. When we had got some little distance from the Fram, we heard a terrible row in front, and presently saw a great brute coming straight toward us, closely followed by the dogs. No sooner did we see what it was than we set off for the ship as fast as we could. Mogstad had his Lappish moccasons on, and knew the way better than I did, so he got to the ship before me; for I couldn't go very fast with these heavy wooden shoes, you see. I missed my way, I suppose, for I found myself on the big hummock to the west of the ship's bows. There I took a good look round, to see if the bear was after me. But I could not see any signs of it, so I started off again, but fell down flat on my back among the hummocks. Oh, yes, I was soon up again, and got down to the level ice near the ship's side, when I saw something coming at me on the right. At first I thought it was one of the dogs; for it isn't so easy to see in the dark, you know. But I hadn't much time for thinking, for the brute jumped right on me, and bit me here, on the side.

I had lifted my arm up like this, you see, and then he bit me on the hip, growling and foaming at the mouth all the while."

"What did you think then, Peter?" asked Nansen.

"What did I think? Why, I thought it was all up with me. I hadn't any weapon, you see; so I took my lantern and hit the beast as hard as ever I could with it on the head, and the lantern broke, and the pieces went skimming over the ice. On receiving the blow I gave him he squatted down and had a good look at me; but no sooner did I set off again than up he got too, whether to have another go at me, or what for, I can't say. Anyhow, he caught sight of a dog coming along, and set off after it, and so I got on board."

"Did you call out, Peter?"

"I should think I did! I holloaed as loud as ever I could!"

And no doubt he did, for he was quite hoarse.

"But where was Mogstad all the while?" asked Nansen.

"Why, you see, he had got to the ship long before me. It never occurred to him, I suppose, to give the alarm; but he takes his gun off the cabin wall, thinking he could manage by himself. But his gun wouldn't go off, and the bear might have had plenty of time to eat me up right under his very nose."

On leaving Peter, the bear, it seems, had set off after the dogs; and it was in this way it came near the ship, where, after killing one of the dogs, it was shot.

In the course of the winter Sverdrup set up a bear-trap of his own invention, but it did not prove very successful. One evening, a bear was seen approaching the trap; it was a bright moonlight night, much to Sverdrup's delight. On reaching the trap, the bear reared itself on its hind legs very cautiously, laid his right paw on the woodwork, stared for a little while at the tempting bait, but didn't seem to approve altogether of the ugly rows of teeth around it. Shaking his head suspiciously, he lowered himself on all fours, and sniffed at the steel wire fastened to the trap, and once more shook his head as if to say, "Those cunning beggars have planned this very carefully for me, no doubt." Then he got up again on his hind legs and had another sniff, and down again on all fours, after which he came toward the ship and was shot.

Autumn passed away and Christmas arrived while the Fram was drifting between seventy-nine and eighty-one degrees north latitude. This tedious drifting was a sore trial to Nansen. He often thought that there must be some error in his calculations, often very nearly lost heart. But then he thought of those at home who had made such sacrifices for him, and of those on board who placed such implicit faith in him; while overhead the star—his star—shone out brilliantly in the wintry night, and inspired him with renewed courage.

The time was now drawing near when their first Christmas on board should be kept. The polar night, with its prolonged darkness and biting cold, brooded over the ship, and ice-pressures thundered all around.

Christmas Eve was ushered in with -35° Fahrenheit. The Fram lay in seventy-nine degrees, eleven minutes, north latitude, two minutes farther south than was the case a week before.

There was a peculiar feeling of solemnity on board. Every one was thinking of home, and trying at the same time to keep his thoughts to himself, and so there was more noise and laughter than usual. They ate and they drank and made speeches, and the Christmas presents were given out, and the Framsjaa, the Fram's newspaper, with an extra illustrated Christmas number, appeared.

In *the* poem for the day it said:—

"When the ship is hemmed in by ice fathom-thick,
   When we drift at the will of the stream,
When the white veil of winter is spread all around,
   In our sleep of our dear home we dream.
Let us wish them a right merry Christmas at home,
   Good luck may the coming year bring;
We'll be patient and wait, for the Pole we will gain,
   Then hurrah for our home in the spring."

The *menu* for Christmas Eve was:—

1. OXTAIL SOUP.
2. FISH PUDDING.
3. REINDEER-STEAK AND GREEN PEAS. FRENCH BEANS, POTATOES, AND HUCKLEBERRY JELLY.
4. CLOUDBERRIES AND CREAM.
5. CAKE AND MARZIPAN.
6. BEER.

The Nansen lads knew how to live. But this night they had no supper; they simply could not manage it. Indeed, it was all they could do to get through an extra dessert, consisting of pineapple preserve, honey-cakes, vanilla biscuits, cocoa macaroons, figs, raisins, almonds, etc.

The banquet was held in their cosey saloon, which was lighted with electric lights; and in the evening they had organ recitals, songs, and many other recreations. Yes, there was merriment galore on the Fram, frozen in though she was in the Polar sea.

If it had not been for the noise of the ice-pressures they might indeed have imagined themselves to be in the very middle of civilization. In their inmost hearts they longed for a pressure,—a pressure of the hand from dear ones at home. A long time must elapse before that could be.

Then came New Year's Eve, with a brilliant aurora shining overhead, and still each one on board felt that irrepressible longing in his heart.

Nansen read out on this occasion the last salutation he had received from Norway. It was a telegram from Professor Moltke Moe at Tromsö:—

> "Luck on the way,
> Sun on the sea,
> Sun in your minds,
> Help from the winds.
> Wide open floes
> Part and unclose
> Where the ship goes.
> Onward! Good cheer!
> Tho' ice in the rear
> Pack—it will clear.
> Food enough—strength enough—
> Means enough—clothes enough.
> Then will the Fram's crew
> Reach the Pole in months few.
> Good luck on thy journey to thee and thy hand,
> And a good welcome back to the dear Fatherland!"

These lines, needless to say, were received with great acclamation.

Meanwhile month after month passes without much change. The men on the Fram live their lonely lives. They take observations in the biting frost—Scott Hansen usually attends to this work. The others, who are sitting down in the cabins, often hear a noise of feet on the deck, as if some one were dancing a jig.

"Is it cold?" asks Nansen, when Hansen and his assistants come below.

"Cold? oh, no! not at all!—quite a pleasant temperature!" a piece of information which is received with shouts of laughter.

"Don't you find it cold about the feet either?"

"No, can't say I do; but every now and then it's rather cool for one's fingers!" He had just had two of his frostbitten.

One morning, indeed, when an observation had to be taken in a hurry, Scott Hansen was seen on deck with nothing on but his shirt and trousers when the thermometer registered -40° Fahrenheit.

Occasionally they would have to go out on the ice to take observations, when they might be seen standing with their lanterns and tackle, bending over their instruments, and then all at once tearing away over the ice, swinging their arms like the sails of a windmill; but it was always, "Oh! it's not at all cold! Nothing to speak of!"

On Friday, Feb. 2, the Fram reached eighty degrees north latitude, an event that was duly celebrated on board. They were all, moreover, in wonderful spirits, especially as the gloom of winter was beginning to lighten at the approach of spring.

By March 23 they had again drifted to the south, and it was not till April 17 that they reached 80° 20' north latitude. On May 21, it was 81° 20', one degree further north, and on June 18, 81° 52'. They were progressing! But after this a back drift set in, and on Sept. 15, 1894, the Fram lay in 81° 14' north latitude.

The weather had been tolerably fine during the summer; but there was little else for them to do except take observations, ascertain the temperature of the water at different depths, etc., and collect specimens of sea-weed, etc. And so another winter with its gloom and darkness was approaching.

During this summer Nansen had often contemplated the idea of leaving the Fram, and of going with one of his companions on a sleigh expedition to the regions nearer the Pole; for he feared the Fram would not drift much farther in a northerly direction, and was most unwilling to return home without first having done his utmost to explore the northern regions. Accordingly he occupied himself a good deal in making sleigh excursions in order to get the dogs into training, and in other preparations. He had mentioned his plan to Sverdrup, who quite approved of it.

About the middle of September a rather strange thing happened. Peterson, who was acting as cook that week, came one day to Nansen, and said he had had a wonderful dream. He dreamt that Nansen intended to go on an expedition to the Pole with four of the men, but would not take him with them.

"You told me," he said, "you wouldn't want a cook on your expedition, and that the ship was to meet you at some other place; anyhow, that you would not return here, but would go to some other land. It's strange what a lot of nonsense one can dream!"

Nansen replied that perhaps it was not such great nonsense, after all; whereon Petersen said, "Well, if you do go, I would ask you to take me with you; I should like it very much! I can't say I am a good hand on ski, but I could manage to keep up with the rest." When Nansen remarked that such an expedition would be attended with no little danger, one involving even the risk of life; "Psha!" answered Petersen, "one can but die once! If I were with you I shouldn't be a bit afraid!" And that he would willingly have accompanied Nansen to the North Pole in the middle of the dark winter, without the slightest hesitation, is sure enough. And so, indeed, would all the others have done.

On Monday, Nov. 19, Nansen mentioned his scheme to Johansen, whom he had selected to be his companion, and on the following day he took the rest of the crew into his confidence. They evinced the greatest interest in the proposed scheme, and, indeed, considered it highly necessary that such an expedition should take place.

And now they all set to work in earnest about the necessary preparations, such as making sleighs, kayaks, exercising the dogs, and weighing out provisions, etc.

Meanwhile winter dragged on its weary way. Another Christmas came, finding them in latitude, eighty-three degrees, and ice pressures were increasing daily. The New Year of 1895 was ushered in with wind, and was dark and dreary in the extreme. On Jan. 3, the famous ice-pressure occurred, that exposed the Fram to the severest strain any ship ever encountered, and lived.

At 8 A.M. on the morning of the 3d of January Nansen was awakened by the familiar sound of an approaching pressure. On going up on deck he was not a little surprised to see a huge pressure-ridge scarcely thirty paces away from the Fram, with deep cracks reaching almost to the ship itself. All loose articles were at once stowed away on board. At noon the pressure began again, and the dreaded ridge came nearer and nearer. In the afternoon preparations were made to abandon the ship, the sleighs and kayaks being placed ready on deck. At supper-time it began crunching again, and Nordahl came below to say that they had better go up on deck at once. The dogs, too, had to be let loose, for the water stood high in their kennels.

During the night the ice remained comparatively quiet, but next morning the pressure began again. The huge ridge was now only a few feet from the ship.

At 6.30 Jan. 5 Nansen was awakened by Sverdrup telling him that the ridge had now reached the ship, and was level with the rails. All hands at once rushed on deck; but nothing further occurred that day till late in the evening, when the climax came. At eight P.M. the crunching and thundering was worse than ever; masses of ice and snow dashed over the tent and rails amidships. Every one set to work to save what he could. Indeed, the crashing and thundering made them think doomsday had come; and all the while the crew were rushing about here and there, carrying sacks and bags, the dogs howling, and masses of ice pouring in every moment. Yet they worked away with a will till everything was put in a place of safety.

When the pressure finally was over, the Fram's port-side was completely buried in the ice-mound; only the top of the tent being visible. But she had stood the trial—passed through it gloriously; for she came out of it all uninjured, without even a crack. There she lay as sound as ever, but with a mound of ice over her, higher indeed than the second ratline of her fore-shrouds, and six feet above the rails.

# Chapter IX

Nansen and Johansen start on a Sleighing Expedition.—Reach Eighty-six Degrees, Fourteen Minutes, North Latitude.—Winter in Franz Joseph's Land.

March 17, 1895, was a memorable day in the Fram's history, for it was on that date that Nansen and Johansen set out on the most adventurous expedition ever undertaken in the polar sea. At the time of leaving the ship, she was in eighty-four degrees north latitude.

On quitting her they fired a salute on board with all their guns as a farewell; and, though the lads on the Fram kept their spirits up bravely, every eye was full of tears, something quite uncommon with them: and they watched their two adventurous comrades, with their sleighs and dogs, as they set off toward the Pole, till they were lost to sight among the hummocks.

The ice was terribly difficult, and they had a wearisome march over it; and, to make matters worse, a southerly drift set in, driving them nearly as far back as they advanced. However, they got on pretty well till reaching eighty-five degrees north latitude, when another back drift set in, lasting, indeed, without intermission during the whole of the expedition. The dogs, too, got worn out, and had to be killed one after the other; while, to add to their discomfort, their clothes would get frozen so stiff during the day that they had to thaw them in their sleeping-bags at night with the warmth of their bodies. Very often they were so tired in the evening that they would fall asleep with the food in their hands. Their expedition, too, haunted them in their sleep; and often Nansen would be awakened by hearing Johansen call out in the night, "Pan!" "Barabbas!" or "The whole sleigh is going over!" or "Sass-sass," "Prr!" Lappish words to make the dogs quicken their pace or to halt.

*Nansen and Johansen leaving the Fram*

It was sorrowful work to have to kill these faithful animals when they were worn out. Nansen himself says that he often felt the bitterest self-reproaches, and confessed that this expedition seemed to destroy all the better feelings of his nature. But forward they must go, and forward they went, though their progress was very slow.

It was not long before Nansen became convinced that it would be an utter impossibility to reach the Pole through such masses of pack-ice and hummocks as they encountered. The question, therefore, was how far they should venture toward it before turning their faces southward.

On Monday, April 8, they had reached eighty-six degrees, ten minutes, north latitude (though it subsequently turned out to be eighty-six degrees, fourteen minutes, north latitude, that renowned degree of latitude that became historical when the news of the Nansen expedition was flashed all over the world), and determined to go on no farther. So, on the day following, they changed their course to the south. The going improved a little as they travelled on. As far as the eye could reach huge masses of ice towered aloft toward the north, while toward the south the ice became each day more favorable, a circumstance that cheered them up not a little.

On Sunday, May 5, they were in eighty-four degrees, thirty-one minutes, north latitude, and on the 17th, in eighty-three degrees, thirty minutes, north latitude.

They found it very hard work crossing the open channels in the ice; and what made it harder was that the number of their dogs diminished daily, one after another having to be killed as food for the survivors. It was absolutely necessary, however, to reach a latitude where game could be procured, before their stock of provisions gave out.

On May 19 they came on the tracks of a bear, but did not see the animal itself. Tracks of foxes they had already seen when in eighty-five degrees north latitude.

It seemed as if there was no end to these channels which must be crossed, and of the young ice which made hauling the sleighs such terribly hard work. Moreover, soon they would have no dogs left to help them, and they would have to drag the sleighs themselves.

May passed and June set in, and still no end to the channels or to their excessive hard work, and not a glimpse of land to be seen yet. Every now and then a narwhal would be seen, or a seal, heralds, doubtless, that they were approaching the regions of animated nature. The ice, too, no longer hard and smooth, became regular slush, so that it clogged on the under surface of their ski, and strained to the utmost the poor dogs, who could hardly drag their loads after them. Everything, indeed, seemed against them! Three months had elapsed since quitting the Fram, and as yet they had met with no change for the better.

On June 16 Kaifas, Haren, and Suggen were the sole survivors of the pack, and Nansen and Johansen had to do dogs' work themselves in dragging the sleighs.

But a turn for the better set in. On the 22d, as they were rowing the kayaks over some open water, they were fortunate enough to shoot a large seal. Its flesh lasted them a good while, and indeed proved a great godsend, though they did set fire to the tent while frying blood pancakes in blubber—a mere trifle, however, on such an expedition as theirs! They soon mended it with one of the sleigh sails, and the blood pancakes were voted to be delicious. On the 24th Nansen shot another seal, an event duly celebrated with great festivity; viz., a supper of chocolate and blubber.

On June 30 Nansen discovered, to his great chagrin, that they had advanced no farther south than they were a month ago, and it began to dawn upon him that in all probability they would have to winter up there—a pleasant prospect, forsooth! Their stock of provisions was nearly exhausted, and only three dogs left.

On July 6 they shot three bears, so that all anxiety as regards food was happily at end for the time; though the prospect of reaching home that year, at least, was infinitesimally small.

On Tuesday, July 23, they finally broke up "Longing Camp," as they termed their quarters, and devoted all their energies to their journey homeward.

The next day they saw land for the first time. Through the telescope its hazy outline could be discerned; but it took them a fortnight to reach it, and when they did reach it, they were so exhausted that they had to lie up several days.

During this time Johansen was nearly killed by a bear. Nansen tells the story:—

"After some very hard work we at last reached an open channel in the ice which we had to cross in our kayaks. I had just got mine ready, and was holding it to prevent its sliding down into the water, when I heard a scuffle going on behind me; and Johansen, who was dragging his sleigh, called out, 'Get your gun!' I looked round, and saw a huge bear dash at him, and knock him down on his back. I made a grab at my gun, which was in its case on the foredeck; but at the same moment my kayak unfortunately slipped down into the water. My first impulse was to jump in after it, and shoot from the deck; but it was too risky a venture to attempt, so I set to work to haul it up on the ice again as quickly as I could. But it was so heavy that I had to kneel down on one knee, pulling and hauling and struggling to get hold of the gun, without even time to turn around and see what was going on behind me. Presently I heard Johansen say very calmly, 'If you don't look sharp, it will be too late.' Look sharp! I should think I did look sharp! At last I got hold of the butt-end of the gun, drew it out of its case, whipped round in a sitting posture, and cocked one of the barrels which was loaded with shot. Meanwhile the bear stood there scarcely a yard away from me, and was on the point of doing for Kaifas. I had no time to cock the other barrel, so I gave it the whole charge of shot behind the ear, and the brute fell dead between us.

"The bear must have followed on our tracks like a cat, and hiding behind blocks of ice, have slunk after us while we were busy clearing the loose ice away in the channel, with our backs turned toward it. We could see by its tracks that it had wormed its way on its stomach over a ridge in our rear, under cover of an ice-mound in close proximity to Johansen's kayak.

"While Johansen, without of course suspecting anything, or even looking behind him, was stooping down to lay hold of the hauling-rope, he got a glimpse of some animal lying in a crouching posture at the stern of the kayak. He thought at first it was only the dog Suggen; but before he had time to notice how large it was, he received a blow over the right ear that made him 'silly,' and over he went on his back. He now tried to defend himself the best he could with his bare fists, and with one hand gripped the brute by the throat, never once relaxing his hold.

"Just as the bear was about to bite him on the head, he uttered those memorable words, 'Look sharp!' The bear kept watching me intently, wondering no doubt what I was up to, when all at once it happily caught sight of one of the dogs, and immediately turned toward it. Johansen now let go his hold of the brute's throat, and wriggled himself away, while the bear gave poor Suggen a smack with his paw that made him howl as he used to do when he got a thrashing. Kaifas, too, got a smack on the nose. Meanwhile Johansen had got on his feet, and just as I fired had got hold of his gun, which was sticking up out of the hole in the kayak. The only damage done was that the bear had scraped a little of the grime and dirt off Johansen's right cheek, so that he goes with a white stripe on it now, besides a scratch on one hand. Kaifas, too, had his nose scratched."

On reaching land they had to shoot Kaifas and Suggen, the sole survivors of their twenty-six faithful companions. It was a hard task. Johansen took Nansen's dog Kaifas in a leash behind a hummock, while Nansen did the same with Johansen's Suggen. Their two guns went off simultaneously, and the two men stood friendless, alone in the desert of ice. They did not say many words to each other on meeting.

---

Along the coast of the land they discovered there was open water, of which they availed themselves, first lashing their kayaks together so that they formed in fact a double kayak.

They rowed for several days, and were fortunate enough to shoot a walrus; but they had no idea what land it was, or where they were.

One evening, however, the channel closed up, and no more open water was to be found. But on Aug. 13 it opened up again, and they were able to push on. After twenty-four hours it closed once more, and they had to drag the kayaks on the sleigh overland. On the evening of Aug. 18 they reached one of the islands they had been steering for, and for the first time for two years had bare earth under their feet. Here they revelled in "the joys of country life,"—now jumping over the rocks, or gathering moss and specimens of the flora, etc.,—and hoisted the Norwegian flag.

In its summer dress this northern land seemed to them to be a perfect paradise; plenty of seals, sea-birds, flowers, and mud—and in front the blue sea.

They were, therefore, loath to leave it, but onward they must proceed, if they wished to reach home that autumn. But fate willed it otherwise.

They soon encountered ice again—nothing but ice—bare ice as far as the eye could reach. After waiting a considerable time, they once more had open water, of which they took advantage by hoisting a sail; but at the end of twenty-four hours their course was again blocked—a block that decided their future movements materially; for they were compelled to winter there!

It may readily be supposed that this was not only a terrible disappointment, but a severe trial to our two arctic navigators. After all their labor and exertion, after reaching open water, and buoying themselves up, with the hope that their struggles would soon be over, to find that hope shattered, and their plans rendered abortive, and that they must perforce be imprisoned in the ice for months, was enough to make them lose heart altogether. But when once they realized their position, they acted like men, and set to work to build a stone hut, on the roof and floor of which they stretched bear hides. They succeeded in shooting several walruses, the blubber of which provided them with fuel, so that they might have been in a worse plight than they were. Still, it was not altogether pleasant to have to lie in a stone hut during a polar winter, with the thermometer down to -40 Fahrenheit, without any other food than bears' flesh and blubber. Indeed, it required the constitution of a giant to endure it, and unyielding determination not to lose heart altogether.

By working for a week, they finished the walls of their abode, and after getting the roof on, moved into it. They made a great heap of blubber of the walruses they shot outside the hut, covering it over with walrus hides. This was their fuel store. It served of course to attract bears, which was an advantage; and many a one paid the penalty of his appetite by being shot. At first they found it very uncomfortable at night, so they both slept in one sleeping-bag, and thus kept tolerably warm. But the climax of their joy was building in the roof a chimney of ice to let out the smoke of their fire. They had no other materials to make it out of. It answered capitally, however, having only one drawback; viz., that it readily melted. But there was no lack of ice for making another.

Their cuisine was simple in the extreme, and strangely enough they never got tired of their food. Whatever came to hand, flesh or blubber, they ate readily, and sometimes, when a longing for fatty food, as was often the case, came over them, they would fish pieces of blubber out of the lamps, and eat them with great relish. They called these burnt pieces biscuits; and "if there had only been a little sugar sprinkled on them, they would have tasted deliciously," they said.

During the course of this winter the foxes proved very troublesome. They gnawed holes in the roof, stole instruments, wire, harpoons, and a thermometer. Luckily they had a spare one, so that the register of the temperature did not suffer. They were principally white foxes that visited them; but occasionally they saw the blue fox, and would dearly have liked to shoot some specimens of that beautiful animal, only that they feared their ammunition would not hold out. They shot their last bear on Oct. 21, after which they saw no more till the following spring.

It was a long, tedious winter; the weather generally very boisterous, with drifting snowstorms. But every now and then fine weather would set in, when the stars would shine with great brilliancy, and wondrously beautiful displays of the aurora borealis would lighten up the whole scene.

Another Christmas Eve arrived, the third they had spent in the polar regions; but this was the dreariest and gloomiest of them all. However, they determined to celebrate it, which they did by reversing their shirts. Then they ate fish-meal with train-oil instead of butter, and for a second course toasted bread and blubber. On Christmas morning they treated themselves to chocolate and bread.

On New Year's Day, 1896, there were -41° of cold (Fahrenheit), and all Nansen's finger-tips were frost-bitten. Out there on that dreary headland their thoughts wandered away to their home, where they pictured to themselves all the Christmas joy and festivity that would be taking place, the flakes of snow falling gently out-of-doors, and the happy faces of their dear ones within.

> "The road to the stars is long and heavy!"

---

Nansen and Johansen slept during the greater part of that long winter. Sometimes, like bears in their winter quarters, they would sleep for twenty-four hours at a stretch, when there was nothing particular to be done. Spring, however, returned at last, and the birds began to reappear on their northerly flight. The polar bears, too, revisited their hut, so they got plenty of fresh meat. The first bear they killed acted very daringly. Johansen was on the point of going out of the hut one day, when he started back, crying out, "There's a bear just outside!" Snatching up his gun, he put his head out of the door of the hut, but instantly withdrew it. "It is close by, and means coming in." Then he put his gun out again, and fired. The shot took effect, and the wounded beast made off for some rocky ground. After a long pursuit Nansen came up with it, and shot it in a snowdrift. It rolled over and over like a ball, and fell dead close to his feet. Its flesh lasted them six weeks.

On May 19 they broke up their winter camp, and proceeded over the ice in a southerly direction, meeting with long stretches of level young ice, making also good use of their sail, and finally reached open water on Friday, June 12. They now lashed the two kayaks together, forming a double kayak, and set out to sea with a favorable breeze, feeling not a little elated; and in the evening lay to at the edge of the ice to rest, having first moored the kayaks with a rope, and then got up on a hummock to reconnoitre. Presently Johansen was heard to shout out, "The kayaks are adrift!" Down they both of them rushed as fast as they could.

"Here, take my watch!" cried Nansen, handing it to Johansen, while he divested himself of his outer garments, and jumped into the water.

Meanwhile the kayaks had drifted a considerable distance. It was absolutely necessary to overtake them, for their loss meant—death.

But we will let Nansen tell the story:—

"When I got tired, I turned over on my back, and then I could see Johansen walking incessantly to and fro on the ice. Poor fellow! he could not stand still; he felt it was so dreadful to be unable to do anything. Moreover, he did not entertain, he told me, much hope of my being able to reach them. However, it would not have mended matters had he jumped in after me. They were the worst minutes, he said, he had ever passed in all his life.

"But when I turned over again and began swimming once more, I saw that I was perceptibly gaining on the kayaks, and this made me redouble my exertions. My limbs, however, were now becoming so numb and stiff that I felt I couldn't go on much longer. But I wasn't far off the kayaks now; if I could only manage to hold out a little longer, we were saved—and on I went. My strokes kept getting shorter and feebler every instant, but still I was gaining, and hoped to be able to come up with them. At last I got hold of a ski that lay athwart the bows, and clutched onto the kayaks. We were saved! but when I tried to get aboard, my limbs were so cold and stiff that I couldn't manage it. For a moment I feared it was too late after all, and that although I had got thus far, I should never be able to get on board. So I waited a moment to rest, and after a great deal of difficulty, succeeded in getting one leg up on the edge of the sleigh that was lying on the deck, and so got on board, but so exhausted that I found it hard work to use the paddle."

When Nansen at last got the kayaks back to the edge of the ice, he changed his wet clothes, and was put to bed on the ice, that is to say, in the sleeping-bag, by Johansen, who threw a sail over him, and made him some warm drink, which soon restored the circulation. But when he told Johansen to go and fetch the two auks he had shot as he was rowing the kayaks back, the latter burst out laughing, and said, "I thought you had gone clean mad when you shot."

On Monday, June 15, Nansen's life was a second time in jeopardy. They were rowing after walruses, when one of the creatures bobbed up close by Nansen's kayak, and stuck its tusks through the side. Nansen hit it over the head with the paddle, whereon the brute let go his hold and disappeared.

But the kayak very nearly foundered, and was only hauled up on the ice as it was on the point of sinking.

This was the last perilous adventure on this marvellous expedition.

# Chapter X

Meeting with Jackson.—Return to Norway on the Windward.—
Fram Returns to Norway.—Royal Welcome Home.

It was June 17, Henrik Wergeland's[1] birthday. Nansen had been down to the edge of the ice to fetch some salt water, and had got up on a hummock in order to have a good look about. A brisk breeze was blowing off land, bearing with it the confused sound of bird-cries from the distant rocks. As he stood listening to these sounds of life in that wild desert, which he thought no human eye had ever seen, or human foot trodden before, a noise like the bark of a dog fell on his ear. He started with amazement.

Could there be dogs here? Impossible! He must have been mistaken. It must have been the bird-cries! But no—there it was again! First a single bark, then the full cry of a whole pack. There was a deep bark, succeeded by a sharper one. There could be no doubt about it! Then he remembered that only the day before he had heard a couple of reports resembling gunshots, but had thought it was only the ice splitting and cracking. He now called to Johansen, who was in the tent.

"I can hear dogs over yonder!" he said.

Johansen, who was lying asleep, jumped up and bundled out of the tent. "Dogs?" No! he could not take that in; but all the same went up and stood beside Nansen to listen. "It must be your imagination!" he said. He certainly had on one or two occasions, he said, heard sounds like the barking of a dog, but they had been so drowned in the bird-cries that he did not think much of it. To which Nansen replied that he might think what he liked, but that for his part he intended to set out as soon as they had had breakfast.

So it was arranged that Johansen should stay there to see to the kayaks, while Nansen set out on this expedition.

Before finally starting, Nansen once more got up on the hummock and listened, but could hear nothing. However, off he started, though he felt some doubts in his own mind. What if it were a delusion after all?

*Meeting of Nansen and Jackson*
*By Permission of Harper & Brothers.*

After proceeding some distance he came on the tracks of an animal. They were too large to be those of a fox, and too small for a wolf. They must be dog tracks, then! A distant bark at that moment fell on his ear, more distinct than ever, and off he set at full speed in the direction of the sound, so that the snow dust whirled up in clouds behind him, every nerve and muscle of his body quivering with excitement. He passed a great many tracks, with foxes' tracks interspersed among them. A long time now elapsed during which he could hear nothing, as he went zigzagging in among the hummocks, and his heart began to sink at every step he took. Suddenly, however, he thought he could hear the sound of a human voice—a strange voice—the first for three years! His heart beat, the blood flew to his brain, and springing up on the top of a hummock, he hallooed with all the strength of his lungs. Behind that human voice in the midst of this desert of ice stood home, and she who was waiting there!

An answering shout came back far, far off, dying away in the distance, and before long he discerned some dark form among the hummocks farther ahead. It was a dog! But behind it another form was visible—a man's form!

Nansen remained where he was, rooted to the spot, straining eyes and ears as the form gradually drew near, and then set off once more to meet it, as if it were a matter of life and death.

They approached each other. Nansen waved his hat; the stranger did the same.

They met.

That stranger was the English arctic traveller, Mr. Jackson.

They shook hands; and Jackson said,—

"I am delighted to meet you!"
N. "Thanks; so am I."
J. "Is your ship here?"
N. "No."
J. "How many are you?"
N. "I have a companion out yonder by the edge of the ice."

As they walked along together, Jackson, who had been eyeing Nansen all the while intently, all at once halted, and staring his companion full in the face said,—

"Are not you Nansen?"

"Yes, I am."

"By Jove! I am glad to meet you!"

And he shook Nansen by the hand so heartily as well nigh to dislocate his wrist, his dark eyes beaming with delight. Endless questions and answers took place between them till they reached Jackson's camp, where some of the men were at once despatched to fetch Johansen.

Life with Jackson was for our two northmen a life of uninterrupted comfort and delight. First of all they were photographed in their "wild man's attire;" then they washed, put on fresh clothes, had their hair cut, enjoyed the luxury of a shave; undergoing all the changes from savage to civilized life—changes that to them were inexpressibly delightful. Once more they ate civilized food, lay in civilized beds, read books, newspapers, smoked, drank. What a change after fifteen months of Esquimau fare of blubber and bears' flesh! And yet during all that time they had experienced scarcely a single day's illness.

Jackson's ship, the Windward, was expected to arrive shortly, and it was arranged that Nansen and Johansen should embark on her for Norway.

But our two travellers had to wait a longer time than they anticipated, for it was not till July 26 that the Windward arrived. On Aug. 7, however, they went on board the ship, and steered with a favorable wind for Vardö, where they arrived early in the morning of Aug. 13.

The pilot who came on board did not know Nansen; but when the captain mentioned his name, his old weather-beaten face brightened up, and assumed an appearance of mingled joy and petrified amazement.

Seizing Nansen by the hand, he bade him a thousand welcomes. "Everybody," he said, "had thought him long dead, as nothing had been heard of the Fram."

Nansen assured him he felt no doubt of the safety of the ship, and that he placed as much confidence in the Fram as he did in himself. Otto Sverdrup was in command, and they would soon hear tidings of her.

No sooner had the Windward anchored in Vardö harbor than Nansen and Johansen rowed ashore, and at once repaired to the telegraph office. No one knew them as they entered it. Nansen, thereon, threw down a bundle of telegrams—several hundred in number—on the counter, and begged they might be despatched without delay. The telegraph official eyed the visitors rather curiously as he took up the bundle. When his eye lighted on the word "Nansen," which was on the one lying uppermost, he changed color, and took the messages to the lady at the desk, returning at once, his face beaming with delight, and bade him welcome. "The telegrams should be despatched as quickly as possible, but it would take several days to send them all." A minute later the telegraph apparatus began to tick from Vardö, and thence round the whole world, the announcement of the successful issue of the expedition to the North Pole; and in a few hours' time Nansen's name was on the lips of a hundred millions of people, whose hearts glowed at the thought of his marvellous achievement.

But away yonder in Svartebugta there sat a woman, who would not on that day have exchanged the anguish she had undergone, and the sacrifices she had made, for all the kingdoms of the world.

By an extraordinary coincidence, Nansen met his friend Professor Mohn in Vardö—the man who had all along placed implicit reliance on his theory. On seeing him Mohn burst into tears, as he said, "Thank God, you are alive."

By another equally extraordinary coincidence, Nansen met his English friend and patron, Sir George Baden Powell, in Hammerfest, on his yacht the Ontario, which he placed at Nansen's disposal, an offer which was gratefully accepted. Sir Baden Powell had been very anxious about Nansen, and was, in fact, on the point of setting out on an expedition to search for him, when he thus met him.

That same evening Nansen's wife and his secretary, Christophersen, arrived in Hammerfest, and the whole place was en fête to celebrate the event. Telegrams kept pouring in from all quarters of the globe, and invitations from every town on the coast of Norway to visit them en route.

But the Fram? The only dark spot amid all their joy was that no tidings had been heard of her; and in the homes of those brave fellows left behind there was sadness and anxiety. Even Nansen himself, who had felt so sure that all was well with her, began to feel anxious.

One morning, it was Aug. 20, Nansen was awakened by Sir Baden Powell knocking at his door with the announcement that there was a man outside who wanted to speak to him.

Nansen replied that he was not dressed, but would come presently.

"Come just as you are," answered Sir Baden.

Who could it be?

Hurriedly putting on his clothes, Nansen went down into the saloon. A man was standing there, a telegram in his hand; it was the director of the telegraph office.

He had a telegram, he said, which he thought would interest him, and had brought it himself.

Interest him! There was only one thing in the world that could interest Nansen now, and that was the Fram's fate.

With trembling fingers he tore open the paper, and read,—

Fram arrived in good condition. All well on board. Am going to Tromsö. Welcome home.

O. S.

Nansen felt as if he must fall on the floor; and all he could do was to stammer out, "Fram—arrived!"

Sir Baden Powell, who was standing beside him, shouted aloud with joy, while Johansen's face beamed like the sun, and Christophersen kept walking to and fro; and to complete the tableau, the telegraph director stood between them all, thoroughly enjoying the scene, as he looked from one to the other of the party.

All Hammerfest was en fête, and universal joy was felt the whole world through, when the tidings of the Fram's home-coming were made known.

The great work was ended—ended in the happiest manner, without the loss of a single human life! The whole thing sounded indeed like a miracle. And a miracle the Nansen lads thought it to be when they met Nansen and Johansen in Tromsö; and when all the brave participants in the expedition were once more assembled, theirs was a joy so overwhelming that words fail to describe it.

---

Yes, the great work was ended!

The voyage along the coast began in sunshine and fête. At last, on Sept. 9, the Fram steamed up the Christiania Fjord, which literally teemed with vessels and boats of all sorts, sizes, and descriptions. It was as if some old viking had returned home from a successful enterprise abroad. The ships of war fired salutes, the guns of the fortress thundered out their welcome; while the hurrahs and shouts of thousands rent the air, flags and handkerchiefs waving in a flood of joyful acclamation!

But when with bared head Nansen set foot on land, and the grand old hymn—

"Vor Gud Han Er Saa Fast En Borg"[2]

was sung in one mighty chorus by the assembled multitude, thousands and thousands of men and women felt that the love of their fatherland had grown in their hearts during those three long years,—from the time when this man had set out to the icy deserts of the north, to the moment when he once more planted his foot on his native soil,—a feeling which the whole country shared with them.

To the youth of Norway Fridtjof Nansen's character and achievements stand out as a bright model, a glorious pattern for imitation. For he it is that has recalled to life the hero-life of the saga times among us; he it is that has shown our youth the road to manhood.

*That* is his greatest achievement!

---

1. Henrik Wergeland, Norwegian poet and patriot, born 1808, died 1845.
2. "A mighty fortress is our God."

## About Legatum Publishing

Legatum Publishing strives to produce books and related material with wholesome content for students, parents and children.

It has been said that history is a pact between the dead, the living and the yet unborn. We believe this statement to be true; it is the goal of Legatum Publishing to offer books that will help Europeans and people of European ancestry discover more about their unique history and develop an appreciation for the legacy that they have inherited.

We want to assist parents in granting knowledge to the next generation by providing them with interesting books - including some older titles that are becoming increasingly forgotten or neglected in the modern world.

# Other publications by
# Legatum Publishing

www.legatum-publishing.com

Karl August Schimmer

# The Sieges of Vienna by the Turks

# The Sieges of Vienna by the Turks

In his 1845 work The Sieges of Vienna by the Turks, the Austrian topographer, cultural historian and writer Karl August Schimmer elegantly describes the events of the Siege of Vienna (1529) and Battle of Vienna (1683).

Schimmer identifies how, in both instances, a coalition of European troops fought side by side in order to save Vienna and all of Europe from Ottoman invasion. In 1529 Bohemians, Spaniards and Portuguese were all represented among the city's defenders, and the siege of 1683 saw the famous intervention of King Jan Sobieski's Polish Winged Hussars to prevent Ottoman advancement into Europe.

Schimmer had a goal of promoting patriotism through a colourful writing style. It is our strong belief the book was written to a high scholarly standard. It succeeds in conveying a wide range of information regarding the two wars, especially in contextualising the background that led to the two famous battles, while remaining accessible and engaging to the reader.

For this reason we believe that The Sieges of Vienna by the Turks is an important book for the celebration of our common European history and identity.

Legatum Publishing AS are proud to present this updated reprint, which includes a new foreword, illustrations and a short biography of Karl August Schimmer, giving contemporary readers the opportunity to immerse themselves in these historical events.

# DEFENDERS OF THE GOLDEN APPLE

a children's book about the battle of Vienna by
**Tore Rasmussen**

# Defenders of the Golden Apple,

# by Tore Rasmussen

"Defenders of the Golden Apple – An illustrated history book for kids about the battle of Vienna in 1683" is an educational book about the Battle of Vienna in 1683 for children aged 8-14. It tells the tale of the desperate struggle of the heroic defenders of Vienna against the invading Ottoman Empire. Lasting two months from July to September 1683, the siege brought the city to the brink of collapse.

Vienna, or the "Golden Apple" (its Ottoman nickname), was the jewel in the crown of Europe. The capture of this city would not only have been a military victory for the Ottomans, but a crushing spiritual defeat for Austria and all of Christendom.

This book is also a tale of hope and personal courage. It shows how different parts of Europe came together to unite against a common threat. This historical example gives hope that fraternity among the nations of Europe is possible in times of need.

In this story we find the virtues of bravery, personal responsibility and perseverance in the face of grave dangers and great difficulty. We have chosen a writing style for this book that is exciting and engaging for children to read and to listen to. Through this, we hope to stimulate their curiosity about history; to inspire them to read and explore for themselves.

This book is intended as a work of educational entertainment. While older children and teenagers can easily read it on their own, it is recommended that parents and tutors co-read this book together with the child to enhance their learning experience. The book comes with a complimentary glossary that explains new and difficult words that the child may not yet be familiar with.

# VIENNA 1683

### HENRY ELLIOT MALDEN

# Vienna 1683, by Henry Elliot Malden

Henry Elliot Malden (1849-1931) was honorary secretary of the Royal Historical Society for 30 years and a fellow of the same Institution. In the preface to his book Vienna 1683, published in 1883, exactly 200 years after the Battle of Vienna, Malden writes: "The historical scholar will find nothing new in the following pages; but I have thought it worth while to tell to the general reader a story worth the telling, and to explain not only the details, but the wider bearings also, of a great crisis in European history, no satisfactory account of which exists, I believe, in English, and the two hundredth anniversary of which is now upon us".

It is our firm belief that this book has greater relevance now than ever before. In a time of alarming historical illiteracy and rampant propagandisation of the past, this entertaining and informative account of the events of the siege of Vienna will provide the reader with information and details that are no longer taught by schools and universities across the western world.

Legatum Publishing has therefore decided to reprint this book in 2021, including a new foreword, biography and illustrations. We do this in order to provide the modern reader with a useful and concise tool to better understand the history and importance of 1683's Battle of Vienna; a vital episode in the history of our continent. "Historia magistra vitae" (History is life's teacher), so reads a famous Latin adage, which we hold to be true indeed. We must not forget our history, for without history there is no foundation for culture and without this, there is no future.

138 years have passed since this excellent work was first published and we believe that it is high time for it to receive a new edition. This is but one of many works that are at risk of fading into permanent obscurity and as they pass out of recognition, so too fades a collective sense of our history and roots as Europeans. It is our firm hope that with the republication of this work, we at Legatum Publishing will be making a contribution to the renewal of an awareness and appreciation among Europeans for their own distinct history and identity and that it might help to counteract the efforts of those forces that seek to deny and diminish this, our European legacy.

Lightning Source UK Ltd
Milton Keynes UK
UKHW012029060223
416577UK00001B/154